GROUP GROWERS

From the Editors of
Group Publishing

Loveland, Colorado

Group Growers

Copyright © 1988 by Thom Schultz Publications, Inc.

First Printing

All rights reserved. No part of this book may be reproduced in any manner whatsoever without written permission from the publisher except where noted in the text and in the case of brief quotations embodied in critical articles and reviews. For information write Permissions, Group Books, Box 481, Loveland, CO 80539.

Credits
Edited by Lane Eskew
Designed by Judy Atwood
Illustrations by Martin Bucella, Rand Kruback, Jan Knudson and Alan Wilkes

Scripture quotations are from the Holy Bible, New International Version. Copyright © 1973, 1978, 1984 International Bible Society. Used by permission of Zondervan Bible Publishers.

Library of Congress Cataloging-in-Publication Data
Group growers
    p.   cm.
   ISBN 0-931529-45-X (pbk.)
    1. Church work with teenagers.   2. Church work with youth.
3. Creative activities and seat work. I. Group Books
BV4447.G693 1988   88-15726
259'.23—dc19   CIP

Printed in the United States of America

Contents

Introduction 9
Building Up 11

Blind Trust: *Learn to trust others and build group unity.* 13
The Body Eats Breakfast: *Everyone participates as a particular part of the body.* 14
Bouncing Ball Discussion: *Get a discussion back on its feet with this one.* 16
Candlelight Friendship: *A meaningful time of affirmation.* 16
Christmas Craft Time: *Make Christmas crafts together.* 17
Church Live-In: *Try living together at the church for a week.* 17
Consensus Seeking: *Learn a new decision-making process.* 18
Contemporary Christian Music Raffle: *Host a weekly giveaway.* 19
The Couch Game: *Get to know each other with this game.* 21
Country Banquet: *Activities revolve around a "country" theme.* 21
Daffy Data: *Discover information about new members.* 22
Different Ingredients: *Use cake mix for an object lesson on Christianity.* 23
Domino Unity: *A discussion starter for the subject of group unity.* 24
Drunk Driving Demo: *Show the group what it's like to get caught.* 25
The Envelope, Please!: *A creative communication technique for a presentation.* 26
Family Feud: *Bring parents and group members closer together.* 27
Fifth-Quarter Get-Togethers: *Fun events after home football games.* 28
Five-Minute Worship: *A discussion starter for the topic of worship.* 28
Fruit and Animals: *Use fruit and stuffed animals to get acquainted with each other.* 29
Getting to Know You: *Find out what young people like and what they want to become.* 30
Golden Lips Award: *Handle interruptive kids with this fun idea.* 30
Group Birthday Party: *Celebrate the birth of the youth group.* 31
Guaranteed Win Night: *Everyone wins with this carnivallike discussion starter.* 31
Homework Blues Night: *Build community within the group by helping each other with homework.* 32
How Are You?: *Demonstrate meaningful communication.* 33
How Well Do You Know Me?: *Determine how well friends know each other.* 33
Introducing . . . Me: *Everyone wins friends with this one.* 34
Kangaroo Court: *Break tension within the group.* 35
Kidnap Breakfast: *Drag group members out of bed to have breakfast together.* 35
Kid-Parent Role Reversal: *A fun role play with kids and parents.* 36
A Label on Your Forehead: *Learn to empathize with others.* 38
Leader's Night Off: *Group members take over the meeting.* 38

Light and Love Feast: *A great idea for closing a retreat or special gathering.* **39**
Live Links: *Each person is an important part of the body of Christ.* **40**
Love Letters: *Parents show their love for kids in a surprising way.* **41**
Meatless Dinner: *A discussion starter on hunger and nutrition.* **41**
Merry-Go-Round Mixer: *Kids discover new facts about each other with this mixer.* **42**
Nail Soup: *An activity on group unity.* **43**
Name Game: *Participants have fun with the spiritual meanings of their names.* **43**
Newcomers Night: *Welcome the freshmen into your high school youth group.* **44**
Parent-Kid Talk Show: *Spark discussion between parents and kids.* **45**
Pass the Peas: *An unusual way to build togetherness.* **46**
People Hunt: *An adventuresome way for the group to mix with new members.* **46**
Pillow Talk: *Use pillows as a mode of self-expression.* **47**
Pow-Wow: *Share both good and bad experiences with each other.* **49**
Progressive Variations: *Different ideas for progressive dinners.* **50**
The Puzzle: *Discuss the unique contributions of each individual to the group.* **51**
Puzzle Unity: *Illustrate the importance of group unity with this object lesson.* **52**
Regressive Dinner: *A backward progressive dinner.* **53**
Roller-Skating Reflection Night: *Combine roller-skating and the topic of friendship.* **53**
Song Signs: *A creative song-leading idea for youth Sunday.* **55**
Spaghetti Extravaganza: *Everything is based on the noodle—from the meal to the devotions.* **55**
Staff Trivia: *Unify the youth group adult staff and group members.* **56**
Swap Labor for Fun: *Make an out-of-reach activity affordable.* **57**
Talk Circles: *Improve young people's listening and communicating skills.* **58**
Tinkertoy Communication: *Use Tinkertoys and practice the art of precise communication.* **58**
Tinkertoy Teams: *Learn about non-verbal communication.* **59**
Toilet Paper Confessions: *This crowdbreaker gives people a chance to talk about themselves.* **60**
Traveling Hoagie: *Progressively build a submarine sandwich.* **60**
Trip Journal: *A great idea for summer travels.* **61**
Trip Talk: *Turn a boring bus ride into a group-building experience.* **62**
We Are the Body: *Get everyone involved in this Bible study.* .... **63** ✓
White Shirt Party: *Advertise personal aspects on an old shirt.* **63**
Who Is the Visitor?: *Welcome group visitors by playing this game.* **65**
Whose Secret Is It?: *Guess others' secrets.* **65**
Yarn Circle: *Illustrate cooperation and unity with this object lesson.* **66**

CONTENTS • 5

Growing In 67

100 Percent Chance of Rain: *Group members reveal their priorities.* 69
Americans and Foreigners: *A look at the American lifestyle.* 69
Appreciation Adjectives: *Help kids appreciate each other.* 70
Balloon Confessions: *Individuals explore God's forgiveness.* 71
Balloon Putdowns: *Decrease putdowns and increase compliments.* 71
Bible Study Scavenger: *Combine a Bible study, a scavenger hunt and a show-and-tell session.* 72
Bible Treasure Hunt: *Search for the hidden words of a Bible verse.* 74
The Body: *Look at individual roles within the group.* 75
Body Parts: *A discussion starter on individual parts of the body of Christ.* 76
Books for a Secret Friend: *Secretly show appreciation for each other.* 76
Cassette Tape Recorder Parables: *Make Bible passages come alive.* 77
Christmas Devotion: *Kids explain what Christmas means to them.* 78
Christmas "Gift List" Exchange: *A creative gift-giving exercise.* 78
Clone Party: *Emphasize each person's uniqueness.* 79
Cookie Decorators: *Sugar cookies provide a snack as well as a discussion starter.* 80
Custom Devotionals: *Write devotional guides and share them.* 81
Decision-Making: *Evaluate the process of making decisions.* 82
Designer Jeans: *Affirm others' unique gifts.* 84
Fame: *Explore the difference between fame and what really matters in life.* 84
Food for Food: *A scripture memorization activity.* 85
Footwashing: *A memorable Easter idea.* 86
Forgiveness Test: *Examine attitudes about forgiveness.* 87
Friends During the Week: *An affirmation exercise that lasts all week.* 88
Gift List: *Recognize and value God-given gifts.* 89
Grab Bag Insights: *Encourage individuals to reflect on their lives.* 90
Graduates Banquet: *Host a dinner in honor of graduating seniors.* 90
Heavenly Pass: *Evaluate good works in relation to heaven.* 91
If I Could: *Explain a particular gift given to a group member.* 92
Let God's Light Shine: *Challenge kids to let their lights shine all day long.* 93
Light in the Darkness: *Teach members about being lights in the world.* 94
Living Water: *Explore the topic of Jesus and "living water."* 94
The Lost Coin: *Illustrate the parable of the lost coin and God's concern for kids.* 95
Love Line: *Utilize letter writing to cultivate relationships.* 96
Love Raffle: *Everyone's a winner with this raffle.* 96

Martha-Worries Bag: *Set worries aside.* 97
Meeting in the Dark: *Examine Jesus as the light of the world.* 97
Me Meter: *Avoid self-references the entire meeting.* 98
More Hamburger Than Steak: *Look at the differences in personalities.* 99
Multiplying Money: *Illustrate the parable of the talents.* 100
The New Me: *A New Year's experience on changes within a person's life.* 100
Paper Towel Lessons: *Use artistic talent while learning biblical principles.* 101
People Collages: *Discover impressions of others.* 102
Peter and Peer Pressure: *An object lesson on peer pressure.* 102
Praising Stones: *A colorful illustration on praising God.* 103
Prayer Advocates: *Pray for one another.* 104
Prayer Partners: *Partners pray secretly for each other throughout the year.* 104
Prayer Probe: *Illuminate the meaning of prayer.* 104
Psalm 1, Illustrated: *Make a slide presentation based on Psalm 1.* 105
Question of the Week: *Group members answer each other's questions.* 106
Secret Bible Study: *Simulate a Bible study in a less fortunate nation.* 107
Self-Image Objects: *Help group members learn more about each other and about themselves.* 108
Sense Scriptures: *Visualize and sense a Bible story.* 109
Shopping Mall Adventures: *Probe the various aspects of commercialism and servanthood.* 110
Soap Carving: *Carve a symbol of something important in life.* 110
Spirit Cards: *Discover the fruit of the Spirit.* 111
Stand on Numbers: *Exhibit opinions and strength of feelings.* 112
Symbolic Gifts: *Give gifts that symbolize love for one another.* 112
Talent Match: *A good kickoff for a program on self-esteem.* 113
Thinking of God: *Explore kids' perceptions of God.* 114
This Is Your Life: *Celebrate birthdays with this activity.* 115
Tours for Teenagers: *Investigate various careers.* 116
Two Greatest Commandments: *A meeting that emphasizes loving God and loving one another.* 116
Unemployment Line: *Think about different job positions.* 118
What's Important?: *Evaluate what's really important in life.* 118
You Were There: *Study the Bible in a setting similar to the passage studied.* 119

Reaching Out 121

Action Announcements: *Keep the group interested with this announcement idea.* 123

CONTENTS • 7

Andrew Club: *Increase youth group enthusiasm and attendance.* **123**
Caring Raid: *Show love to someone in need.* **124**
Carnival Can Night: *Obtain canned goods for a service organization by holding a carnival.* **125**
Charity Scavenger Hunt: *Collect useful items for a local or denominational shelter for kids.* **125**
Christmas Card Delivery: *Deliver Christmas cards for free.* **126**
Christmas in July: *Have Christmas in July for a nursing home or rest home.* **127**
Clip Art Album: *Construct your own clip art organizer.* **128**
Commercial Break: *Give announcements via videotape.* **128**
Commercials for Jesus: *Videotape each member's opinion about Jesus.* **129**
Construction Site Art: *A community service project.* **129**
Dollar Bill Giveaway: *Illustrate the ups and downs of sharing faith.* **131**
Double-Duty Giving: *Reach out to parents.* **132**
February Love-In: *A way for the group to show its love to the congregation.* **133**
Garden Outreach: *Grow your own food and donate it to an organization for the needy.* **134**
A Gift of Love: *Evaluate relationships with others.* **135**
Group Greeting Cards: *Make creative greeting cards.* **136**
Halloween Treat Night: *Give treats and friendship to the older and shut-in people in the community.* **137**
High-Tech Slides: *Produce creative slides for announcement time.* **137**
Hunger Game: *Look at the complexities of world hunger.* **138**
Hunger Service: *Sponsor a youth-led service on world hunger.* **138**
Jail House Blues: *Attract new members and learn new information about the regulars.* **139**
Love Songs: *Get inactive members back in the youth group.* **140**
Map for Lost Members: *Send a funny map to an inactive member.* **141**
Mirror Messages: *A creative way to advertise an event.* **142**
Newsletter Pizza Contest: *Gain more interest in the youth group newsletter.* **142**
Nursing Home Pet Show: *Bring pets to a nursing home.* **143**
Outdoor Easter Decorations: *Decorate the community for Easter.* **144**
Palm Sunday Fair: *Learn more about Lent and Holy Week with these events.* **145**
Pantry Raid: *A zany way to collect food for distribution to the needy.* **146**
Phone Devotions: *Receive calls for recorded devotional messages.* **147**
Photo Revue: *Assign someone to take crazy photographs of the group.* **147**
Photo Teams: *Various imaginative photography techniques.* **148**
Pizza Pig-Out: *Build attendance with this get-together.* **149**
Poster Day: *Photograph your group and make a poster.* **150**
Progressive Publicity: *Increase interest with this publicity idea.* **151**

Publicity Posters: *Arouse curiosity with posters.* **151**
Pumpkin Symbols: *Display meaningful symbols carved in pumpkins.* **152**
Reasons or Excuses?: *Ignite a discussion on church attendance.* **152**
Roster: *An effective tool for youth group unity.* **153**
Roving Photo Screens: *Utilize cardboard and a projector for a fun performance.* **154**
Santa's Secret Service: *Surprise a special family with gifts.* **155**
Signed, Anonymous: *Build suspense for upcoming events.* **156**
Snapshot Browser: *Put together a youth group photo album.* **156**
Sofa Stuff: *Increase attendance with this game.* **156**
Sponsor a Child: *Provide support for a child in need.* **157**
Superminute: *Record what Easter means to kids for your next Easter service.* **158**
Tree Santas: *Give Christmas trees to needy families.* **159**
Trick-or-Treat Reversed: *Give candy while Christmas caroling.* **160**
Tutor Service: *Help elementary-age kids with their homework.* **160**
"Who's His" News: *Boost youth group morale with a regular news section in the church bulletin or newsletter.* **161**
Youth Breakfast Week: *Invite churches from all over for this grand event.* **162**

Your Ideas Wanted 163

Contributors to Group Growers 165

INTRODUCTION

Why are new ideas hard to think of when you need them the most? To help meet the never-ending need for new activities, GROUP Magazine created the "Try This One" section. In "Try This One," youth group members and leaders from across the country submit meaningful, successful and original activities that work in their groups.

Group Growers is a compilation of fun, meaningful and lively activities that help your group members grow closer to each other, grow individually and reach out to those outside the group. You'll also discover creative ideas for publicizing events and promoting the group.

You'll find three sections:

● Building Up—growth as a group, with themes such as unity, friendship and communication.

● Growing In—individual and spiritual growth, with themes such as affirmation, worship and gifts.

● Reaching Out—involving activities that range from service projects to attendance-building ideas.

Flip through the following pages until you find a fun game or activity that meets your programming needs. Inspire unity, spiritual growth and compassion among your group members. Be creative. Adapt, modify and enlarge the activities for your group's enjoyment. If you come up with a new idea—great! Send it to us. See "Your Ideas Wanted" on page 163 for more details.

Building Up

BLIND TRUST

This exercise is especially effective in building group unity and trust.

Everyone stands together in a large circle in an area free from any obstructions. One member of the group stands in the center and becomes the "walker." The walker holds his or her arms straight out, with eyes closed tight. The walker then spins in place two or three times and then starts walking straight ahead without opening his or her eyes.

When the walker approaches one of the members standing in the circle, that member then moves forward, grasps an arm, and swings the walker around and lets him or her go back in toward the center of the circle. The walker keeps moving in that direction, blind to any orientation, until a member at the opposite side of the circle grasps an arm and swings him or her back again. The process repeats itself for a couple of minutes and then a new walker is chosen.

The objective of this exercise is to keep the blind walker out of harm's way by leading him or her always back into the center. When the group becomes particularly familiar with this exercise, a second walker might be sent in at the same time. With two walkers, however, the outer circle members have to be especially careful where they point the walkers, lest they run into each other and hurt themselves. This is where the element of trust plays an important role. The walker must display confidence in the group members by blindly submitting himself or herself to their rule. The group in turn must be careful not to betray that trust and allow the walker to get hurt.

Each group member should have a chance to be the walker. Just a few minutes of this exercise is bound to bring almost any new group closer together.

THE BODY EATS BREAKFAST

Here's a crazy variation of a skit that will get lots of laughs and also illustrate 1 Corinthians 12:12-30.

Divide your group into teams of six. Have each of the six team members become one of the following body parts:

1. Eyes. This person is the only one in the group who isn't blindfolded. While Eyes can't use his or her arms or talk, he or she can whisper to Mouth and listen to Ears.

2. Ears. Blindfolded and can't use his or her arms or talk, and can only whisper with Mouth and Eyes.

3. Mouth. Blindfolded, can't use arms, repeats only what Ears says to do.

4. Right Arm. Blindfolded, uses Right Arm only upon commands from Mouth.

5. Left Arm. Blindfolded, uses Left Arm only upon commands from Mouth.

6. Legs. Blindfolded, stands on hands and knees between Mouth's legs, moves forward, backward, left or right only on Mouth's commands.

Right Arm, Ears and Left Arm lock arms. Mouth stands behind Ears and hangs on to his or her waist.

Ahead of time, prepare a bowl of shredded wheat and water for each team. Make sure the concoction is super messy before starting the contest. Place the bowls 15 to 20 feet from The Body. (You could also have The Body brush Mouth's teeth.)

BUILDING UP • **15**

The object of the activity is for The Body to move to the bowl of cereal, pick it up, eat the cereal and return to the starting place. Remember Legs? He or she is on hands and knees under Mouth's mouth. Legs will probably get his or her head and shoulders plastered with soggy shredded wheat.

Here's a sample of the action: Eyes tells Ears to tell Mouth to move forward. Mouth tells the rest of The Body to move forward. Eyes tells Ears to turn right or left and to stop. The going can get hilarious when Eyes tells Ears to tell Mouth to tell Right Arm and Left Arm to start feeding

Mouth. (One Arm holds the bowl while the other Arm spoons the food toward Mouth.)

The rules are simple. The Body parts can only perform those functions specifically assigned to them. If The Body breaks apart or starts talking with other parts, the whole body has to start from the beginning again.

After The Body has eaten, you can discuss how each body part felt about being such a small part of The Body. Read 1 Corinthians 12:12-30. Discuss practical applications this passage has for the youth group and for the entire church.

BOUNCING BALL DISCUSSION

Try this one when a discussion appears ready to die. Bounce a red rubber ball back and forth to group members. The person who catches the ball must add a comment to

the discussion. (Limit on speaking time: one minute.) Then the speaker bounces the ball to another member, who adds a comment. Bouncing the ball to the shyer members helps encourage response.

Discussions are more lively and stimulating whenever the ball starts bouncing.

CANDLELIGHT FRIENDSHIP

This activity helps build friendship and unity in a group. It works well with mature teenagers in a retreat or evening setting.

Have everyone sit in a circle on the floor. Light a candle

and turn off the lights. Give the candle to someone to hold; each person should say something that affirms the candle holder's worth. Then the candle moves to the next person in the circle and the process continues. Make sure everyone has a turn holding the candle.

CHRISTMAS CRAFT TIME

Help your young people work on Christmas gifts, have a good time and get to know each other better!

Find out which of your group members like to work on crafts, and arrange for an evening when you and interested kids can get together. Work on Christmas craft projects; group members may want to work on individual gifts or prefer to work together on a big project. They may want to work at different crafts or prefer to make the same craft. Be flexible. Offer special instruction in crafts if members would like to learn new skills or if they need help with their project(s). Group members or adults in your church may be able to teach crafts.

Group members can meet together and learn how to quilt, make pillows and make wall hangings.

Everyone will have a great time.

CHURCH LIVE-IN

Need unity in your group? Try living at the church for a week.

Set goals for the week, and have everybody sign a commitment paper agreeing to live at the church all week.

Move in on a Sunday evening after church.

Each morning eat breakfast together and have a short devotional. After school is a time for fun and doing the jobs around the church. Each member takes turns preparing meals, washing dishes, sweeping the floor and cleaning the

restrooms.

Each evening have a time of sharing and singing. On Monday evening have a special speaker talk on unity. Ask a musical group to perform on Wednesday evening. On Friday evening invite the parents for a potluck supper, games and singing.

Personal relationships and group unity will develop during this week.

CONSENSUS SEEKING

Sometimes it's difficult to maintain a good discussion. One or two people or the leader often end up doing most of the talking. One way to combat this problem and to encourage maximum participation is through Consensus Seeking.

Consensus Seeking can be used in either large or small groups but is more effective with groups of 20 or fewer. No lengthy preparations are needed. Five sheets of paper are the essentials. Letter each sheet in advance with one of the following: "strongly agree," "agree," "neutral," "disagree" and "strongly disagree." Then scatter the sheets over the floor.

Make a statement and have each group member stand on or by the sheet with which he or she most closely agrees. After everyone is in place, each member states his or her reasons for standing on a particular sheet.

After listening to each reason, members of opposing views try to persuade members of other opinions to come over to their side by varying and amending the original statement. When a member hears a statement that changes his or her stand, he or she moves to another sheet that more easily reflects this change. This process continues until all or nearly all of the group is standing by one sign.

Another way of utilizing this method is to have members hold up the signs instead of placing them on the floor. Members then go and stand in front of the sign that best expresses their opinions.

Although Consensus Seeking is useful in sparking discussions, it is not limited to this function. This is also an exciting way to involve your group in planning group activities. Instead of the leader throwing out a statement for group reaction, the members vote on individual suggestions as a starting point. All opinions get aired and the group is able to make use of any expertise in the group. This process takes longer than traditional planning methods, but the final decision is acceptable, at least in part, to all.

Consensus Seeking is not a compromise or a majority vote, but a dynamic method of involving the total group in the decision-making process.

CONTEMPORARY CHRISTIAN MUSIC RAFFLE

Every week or month, give away a cassette tape of a contemporary Christian group or singer you know will fit your young people's musical tastes. Here's how it works:

1. Buy a roll of tickets.
2. Each week, each person who attends a youth group meeting receives a ticket to write his or her name on and turn in.
3. As young people enter the meeting, play the tape that you'll give away.
4. Someone draws a ticket and reads the name on the back.
5. If the person whose ticket was drawn isn't there, draw another ticket.
6. Even though the tickets accumulate from week to week, don't allow anyone to win twice until everyone has won once.
7. Also use the tickets as prizes for crowdbreaker winners.

When you travel somewhere together on a bus, you'll hear more and more contemporary Christian music on group members' tape players.

THE COUCH GAME

This game is a great way for group members to learn one another's names, and it's a lot of fun.

Arrange chairs and a couch in a circle. Put two guys and two girls on the couch. Make sure one chair is empty. Write everyone's name on separate slips of paper. Hand them out, making sure no one tells what

name he or she receives.

The object of the game is for the guys or girls to control the couch. To start, the person to the left of the empty chair calls any group member's name. The person who has the paper with that name (not the person whose name it is) moves to the empty chair and exchanges papers with the person who called the name. The person to the left of the newly vacated chair calls out the next name. This continues until either four guys or four girls are sitting on the couch.

Kids'll have a hilarious time trying to remember one another's names. The game will become a standing contest between the guys and the girls.

COUNTRY BANQUET

Use this banquet to honor adult volunteers and give information about upcoming events.

Invitations ask guests to dress "country" (overalls, checkered shirts and straw hats). Decorate the banquet hall with kerosene lamps, quilts, baskets of apples and potatoes, farm-fresh "aigs," cans of fruit and vegetables, calico stuffed chickens and mountain dew jugs.

As the guests arrive, they receive a packet including sheets of youth news and plans, a bandanna, a clothespin name tag and a knock-knock joke with a number on it.

During the country-style meal, call out numbers of the knock-knock jokes; the people with those jokes must stand and read them to an eager audience.

Following the informational "program" part of the gathering, have "volunteers" star in a country-theme melodrama, created especially for the banquet.

Then challenge small groups to create the longest list of uses for a bandanna.

Plenty of country songs, a short devotion and "Amazing Grace" with a harmonica solo in the middle end the Country Banquet.

DAFFY DATA

When your group acquires some new members, it is often helpful to get some basic information on each individual—name, address and interests. Instead of boring questionnaires, here's a fun way to get the information.

As each person arrives, give him or her a piece of paper, with one or two numbers on it. After everyone has come, divide into two teams, using the numbers on the papers. Explain that the teams will be competing, and the team scoring the most points will win. To get points, each person must answer, in writing, some questions.

Questions should include "What is your full name?" and "What is your telephone number?" as well as goofy questions such as "Have you ever touched a camel?" Decide beforehand (but don't announce) what answers to give points for such as 10 points for the person born closest to June 20, or for the team with the most members who dislike cauliflower. The less logic used in deciding points, the better and funnier. Have the final question worth a lot, so that either team could still have a chance. Maybe this will be the chance for the perpetual loser to become the hero by being the only one to remember a trivial bit of information.

After the contest, collect the papers, and you will have painlessly gathered all the necessary information, plus a whole lot more. And you'll all get a little better acquainted in the process.

DIFFERENT INGREDIENTS

This activity will provide entertainment, Bible study, discussion and refreshment if your group has access to a kitchen.

You will need two cooks, a cake recipe and the ingredients. One cook should have the correct ingredients and the other one should have different, incorrect ingredients. He or she should substitute lard for butter and rock salt for sugar. The lousy cook can also be missing some ingredients and use the wrong measurements . . . anything to add humor to the situation. It's a good idea to have the bad cook use a clear bowl and the good cook use a non-transparent bowl.

The good cook tells how to make the cake and occasionally glances over to see how the bad cook is doing.

Finally, when they are done with the mixing, they both place the ingredients in pans. The good cook places his or her ingredients in a cake pan, and the bad cook places his or her ingredients on a cookie sheet.

Then the cakes are placed in the oven to bake while the group discusses how different ingredients in a person's life can make who he or she is. What does the ingredient of Christ do to a person's life?

When the cakes are finished, you can compare them and, of course, eat the better one.

Here's a recipe that comes straight from the Bible:

4½ cups 1 Kings 4:22
1 cup Judges 5:25b
2 cups Jeremiah 6:20
2 cups 1 Samuel 30:12
2 cups Nahum 3:12
2 cups Numbers 17:8
6 cups Jeremiah 17:11
½ cup Judges 4:19b
2 tablespoons 1 Samuel 14:25
Pinch or more of Leviticus 2:13
Season to taste with 2 Chronicles 9:9
2 teaspoons Amos 4:5

DOMINO UNITY

Here's a good discussion starter on the subject of group

unity.

As everyone enters, each person should take one domino. Hold on to it—it represents you. When everyone has arrived, create a design with the dominoes, with everyone putting his or her domino somewhere in the design. Place the dominoes on end and close enough to each other to make possible a chain reaction of knocking each other down should one of them be toppled over.

Members should take a moment to think about where they are going to put their dominoes in the design—near the center, on the end or wherever.

After the design has been completed, ask members to answer in their own minds how they each fit into the design of the youth group.

After some discussion, have someone knock the dominoes down by gently pushing one of them over. See if they all fall down. If not, draw analogies of the importance of closeness to one another in the group to make the group an effective body for Christ. If they all fall down, consider Hebrews 10:25—"Let us not give up meeting together . . ."

Close with the challenge to invite friends to the group and imagine what kind of design could be made if 10 or 15 more kids were involved.

DRUNK DRIVING DEMO

This holiday party season, get kids' attention. Demonstrate the hazards of drunk driving to your group. Secure the cooperation of the local police department and a teenager for this eye-popping discussion starter.

As the kids arrive at church for a meeting, pretend you've forgotten the keys to the building. Wait outside with the kids while you send someone home for keys. Everyone stands on the church's front lawn when the screech of car tires pierces the air. Here's what happens next.

A new car pulls up and stops in front of the church—followed by a police car with its lights flashing and siren screaming. The police car stops behind the car. Katherine, a looked-up-to senior, steps out of the car. Beer cans clang to

the pavement. The police officer questions Katherine and then has her get into the police car. The kids stare in disbelief. The advisers applaud Katherine and the police officer for a great performance.

Take everyone inside the building. Have the police officer show a film or talk about drunk driving. With this introduction, the kids will have loads of questions.

THE ENVELOPE, PLEASE!

This communication technique can have as many forms as you have ideas. Use it to add a touch of mystery and an atmosphere of involvement. Here's how it works.

When you plan a talk or presentation, plan spots where illustration would be helpful. Before your presentation, hand out specially prepared and numbered envelopes, boxes, paper sacks, etc., to group members.

Then during the presentation, call out the numbers when

you're ready for them. Depending on the nature of your talk, have in the containers the following:

- Symbolic objects or pictures.
- Instructions to read, draw, act out or sing something.
- A cassette tape to play.
- A problem to solve such as how the group can share one stick of gum provided.
- Treats for everyone such as candy and balloons.
- Whatever else would be appropriate to your presentation.

For example, at one point in a talk you could ask, "How do we get to heaven?" After a brief discussion, call out an envelope number. Someone opens it and reveals the mystery object: a key that has "Jesus" inscribed on it.

FAMILY FEUD

Here's a fun idea you can use to climax a four-week seminar on parent-teenager relationships.

Do a takeoff on the old *Family Feud* TV game show. Invite all the young people and their parents. Choose two families as contestant teams. The winning family receives free dinners at a local restaurant.

For an "audience survey group," use a class from a local school, with the cooperation of the teacher. These kids complete a written survey that gives you your "popular opinion" answers for the game.

Here are some of the questions you could use: "What is your father's favorite food?" "What is your mother's favorite treat?" (One wise guy who played this game answered, "My father.") "What do you like most about your parents?"

The game is a lot of fun, and it helps communicate some parent-teenager understanding.

FIFTH-QUARTER GET-TOGETHERS

Football season brings fun and a chance for group members to get involved. And Fifth-Quarter Get-Togethers are a great way to get new kids into your youth group.

Plan two-hour get-togethers after each home football game. Ask local Christian bands to perform, show videos or movies, or play games. Have youth group members bring munchies and soft drinks to share.

If your group is small, ask other local youth groups to get together with you.

FIVE-MINUTE WORSHIP

Here's a discussion starter for the topic of worship.

Divide the group into small group "congregations." Give each young person a card with a description of a person he or she must represent. The small groups each have five minutes to plan a worship service that will include "something for everyone."

Following are suggestions of people for your group members to represent: rock 'n roll musician; 85-year-old widow;

someone who only goes to church on Easter and Christmas; opera singer; computer expert; 5-year-old hyperactive boy; deaf mother; 17-year-old girl who is forced to attend church; farmer who is at his first church service; and 30-year-old single parent.

When the five minutes are up, let the small groups present their worship services to the entire group.

This exercise is both hilarious and a good lead into a Bible study on worship or a planning session for a real worship service.

FRUIT AND ANIMALS

Find out more than just your kids' names with these discussion starters.

Have the kids sit in a circle. Put a pile of stuffed animals in the middle of the circle. (Kids can bring them from home.) See which kid can imitate each animal's sound best. The kids will howl with laughter.

Then ask each kid to tell the group which animal best

represents his or her personality and why.

You can do the same thing with a bowl of fruit; ask, "Which fruit best represents your family?"

Use these items and others to start discussions on self-image, God, the family of God, church, school, family, how's your day—almost anything.

GETTING TO KNOW YOU

A good way to get to know people in your group is to find out what they like and what they want to become.

Have everyone write on a piece of paper the answers to these questions: "What is your favorite food, animal, TV show, hobby and color?" Have members sign their names. Don't let kids see anyone's answers. Collect the answer sheets. Then read the answers to the whole group. Members try to guess whom each set of answers belongs to.

Award a point for each right guess. The person with the most points wins the prize.

GOLDEN LIPS AWARD

If the kids in your youth group are interruptive or talk when they're not supposed to during meetings, try this idea.

Cut a large pair of lips out of yellow posterboard. Print in bold letters across the lips "Golden Lips Award." Each week give this traveling award to the person who's the most quiet during the meeting. Have that person bring back the award the following week and give it to someone else. It's a good idea to have two or three copies of the lips in case someone forgets to bring them back.

Other lip awards could be given such as a Pink Lips Award for the person who smiles the most during the meeting, or a White Lips Award for the "good guy" person who says kind things to other group members.

GROUP BIRTHDAY PARTY

If your youth group has just been started, throw a birthday party to celebrate your new beginning.

Include all the trimmings—birthday cupcakes, balloons, party plates, party cups, party napkins, lots of games and other fun stuff.

Near the end of the party, share a short ceremony of dedication to the group. Give each person a birthday cupcake (one small candle per cupcake). One at a time, each member expresses a wish or hope for the new group. After all have shared, light the candles. In unison say, "So let it be done," and blow out the candles.

Make the birthday party an annual celebration. It will help you remember where you've been, how you've grown and where you're going.

GUARANTEED WIN NIGHT

Everyone wins with this carnivallike discussion starter.

Before the meeting, list on newsprint four quiz questions that relate to the meeting's topic. Choose two easy and two hard questions from the Bible or current events; make sure each question has a definite answer. Also hang a dart board on the wall and stick a strip of tape on the floor to indicate where kids will stand to throw darts. And buy a lot of Gummi Bears.

When group members arrive, give each teenager a 3×5 card and a pencil. Have group members write on their 3×5 cards answers to the questions on the newsprint. When everyone's finished the quiz, give kids the answers and have them write the number of correct answers they have on the top of their cards.

Then have kids each toss one dart at the dart board for each correct answer on their card. Record each person's dart-board points. Give kids one Gummi Bear per point. Give leftover Gummi Bears to the person with the fewest points.

Then use the questions and answers as part of a discussion.

HOMEWORK BLUES NIGHT

Use that common youth experience—homework—to build community in your group.

Set aside one night a week besides the regular youth group meeting for a Homework Blues Night, and have a study session. Set up tables and chairs in the youth meeting room. Ask kids to call ahead if they need help with particular subjects. Then ask adults or college students who are experts in different academic areas to volunteer to help the kids. Most of the time, kids help each other.

Meet from 7 to 8:30 p.m. for study. Take a break at 8:30 for munchies. Have kids take turns bringing chips and soda. Turn up the stereo and have kids let off a little steam. Then at 8:45, have a circle time to tell joys and concerns and pray together.

Advertise the night as a "work" time so kids plan to study when they come.

HOW ARE YOU?

How sincere are we when we greet one another? "How are you?" "Fine." Do we really mean it? Here's a group activity to explore this everyday phenomenon.

Station one of your members or leaders at the door as your group is arriving for a meeting. As people enter, the welcomer should say, "Hi, how are you?" Then, the welcomer or an assistant should write the response of each person on a 3×5 card. Now tape the card on the member.

When everyone has arrived, split the group according to responses. All those with cards reading "okay" will make one group. Those with cards reading "fine" will make another group, etc. Now instruct each group to creatively design a skit on the meaning of "Hello, how are you, goodbye."

Present the skits and discuss them.

Conclude with each member going to other members and *meaningfully* giving a verbal or non-verbal goodbye.

HOW WELL DO YOU KNOW ME?

This game shows how well friends know each other. Divide into pairs. Have one partner from each pair leave the room and the remaining partners sit in a circle.

Give each of these people seven or eight pieces of paper and a pen. Ask the members about the partners absent from the room. Following are examples:

- What piece of your friend's clothing do you like best?
- What is your friend's favorite color, food and animal?
- What do you two discuss a lot?

The members write the answers to each question on a sheet of paper. After the questions have been answered, have the other partners come back into the room and stand behind their partners who are seated. Repeat the questions to the newcomers one at a time. If the pair's answers differ, blow an obnoxious horn. If the answers match, the pair wins 10 points. The friends then change roles and repeat the game.

The pair with the greatest number of points wins the game.

INTRODUCING . . . ME

This idea was originally used at a coffeehouse attended by about 50 young people from four churches.

Give a short pencil and an ordinary 8½ ×11 sheet of notebook paper to each person at the door. Have everyone print on the sheet of paper his or her name (first and last) and his or her favorite activity (hobby, occupation or pastime). Stress that members should be careful to list an activity that they will not be embarrassed to have made known publicly.

People should attempt to introduce themselves to everyone else, taking care to relate the exact information on their papers. The object is to memorize the names and favorite activities of as many people (outside of one's own group) as possible. Encourage the learning of additional information, also; it makes it easier to remember the required information. Besides, the underlying purpose of the game is to give everyone a chance to make new friends. After two people have learned each other's names and favorite activities, they should sign each other's sheet of paper and move on to someone else.

Set a certain time during the evening when introductions can be made.

At some time during the evening people should enter the number of names and favorite activities that they can remember on a chalkboard and write their initials beside their claims.

You might offer first-, second- and third-place door prizes. Albums, tapes, books or posters make good prizes. When you're ready to award the door prizes, have those who entered a claim on the board recite their memorized names and favorite activities (having the corresponding people stand up), beginning with the highest claim. Remember, no one may include the names and activities of people in his or her own group, lest those from larger groups be given an unfair advantage. Also, no claims may be changed once the recital of names and activities begins.

For each correct name *and* activity, a person scores a point. If someone remembers the name but forgets the activity, or vice versa, he or she scores half a point. The top three scorers, of course, win the door prizes.

And everybody wins a bunch of new friends.

KANGAROO COURT

An effective way to head off hard feelings within your group at a retreat or on a trip is to "prosecute" the culprits in a Kangaroo Court.

Three guys in one group splashed three girls while everyone was canoeing on an ice-cold lake. The girls didn't see too much humor in their soaked clothes and soggy cameras. Hostile feelings began to brew.

That evening, back at camp, the leader announced that a Kangaroo Court would be held to properly try and prosecute all guilty parties. From that announcement on, everyone began to view the entire incident with a contagious sense of humor.

The defendants were named. A lawyer for the defense was selected, as was a prosecuting attorney. Formal charges were written and submitted to the judge.

A bailiff and court reporter were appointed. Jurors were screened and sworn in.

By the time the trial began, members were laughing so much that they forgot anyone was ever mad.

The trial, complete with witnesses, cross-examinations and outbursts from the defendants, was hilarious.

The three guys were found guilty, but somehow the judge received the penalty—a pie in the face.

A Kangaroo Court, properly handled, is a great way to settle some group hassles.

KIDNAP BREAKFAST

This is primarily a fun activity but can do a lot for building spirit in a youth group.

Get up at 5:30 on a Saturday morning and use a station wagon or large van to go to the homes of your youth group members to pick them up. The young people have no idea what's up.

Go to the first home and wake up the young person

there and both of you return to the car. Having been so rudely awakened, the young person is eager to do the same to the next person on the route. This is done until all the

members of the group are in the van.

Then take the group to your home where your spouse or other adult volunteer has been making pancakes, bacon, etc., for breakfast.

Each member of the group must come dressed in whatever he or she sleeps in (or with a bathrobe on).

Note: Notify the parents of the youth group so that they will not be surprised when the doorbell rings early in the morning.

KID-PARENT ROLE REVERSAL

You can have great fun with a role-play situation with the kids and parents in your church.

Prepare questions concerning dating, morals, current events, etc. Young people answer as if they're parents. Parents answer as if they're teenagers.

Ask the following questions:
1. How old should you be to date?
2. What time should you be home?
3. Should a 10th-grade girl double-date?
4. Should you date on week nights?
5. Should you make your child go to Sunday school?
6. What do you do on dates besides "park"?
7. How do you feel about teenage drinking?
8. What should you do if you feel your child has the "wrong" friends?
9. How much money should you give your child?
10. How do you resolve conflict with your parents?

Make sure each person speaking stays in his or her role.

A LABEL ON YOUR FOREHEAD

Here's a fun game that's a great crowdbreaker and offers empathy to others' feelings.

Cut strips of paper about an inch wide and 6 inches long. Place a 3-foot-long piece of string or yarn on each strip, taping the string to the paper. On the other side of the paper, write the names of various types of personalities such as introvert, extrovert, shy, obnoxious, lonely, sad and caring.

Then, tie the strings around each kid's head with the label showing on his or her forehead. Make sure no one sees his or her label as it is put on.

Now, have everyone "mill around" in the room, conversing with one another. No one may tell another what his or her label is. But each person is to be treated as a person with the characteristic listed on his or her forehead.

After the milling around period is over, everyone gets to remove his or her label and see it. Then have members discuss how they felt about the way they were treated, and how long it took them to discover who they were. They should also think about how they treated other labeled people.

There are many variations to this game. Try this group of labels: preacher, Jesus freak, atheist, Jew, Christian and agnostic. Or this group: old woman, little sister, rich uncle, mother, father and grandfather.

It's okay to give the same name to more than one kid. Sometimes it's interesting to see how two "lonely" labeled people, for instance, may find each other in the milling around period and enjoy each other's company.

LEADER'S NIGHT OFF

Here's a great way to increase your group members' participation in a meeting and give you a "breather" from your normal role.

Before the meeting, write instructions on individual slips of paper for various segments of the meeting such as "choose and lead songs," "open in prayer," "choose a

Bible passage and read it to the group" and "offer a few thoughts on getting along with parents."

Pass these slips of paper to members as they arrive at the meeting. Allow a few moments for organizing thoughts and the meeting's order. Then, start the session.

You'll be pleased with how well and quickly your group comes up with fresh and creative ideas.

LIGHT AND LOVE FEAST

Use this fine idea to close a retreat or special gathering.

First, give everyone a candle. Share several scriptures about Jesus being "the light of the world." Have a large candle burning near a picture of Christ. Then light your candle from the large candle and share one special word such as "love" or "peace" and what that word means to you. Then spread the light by lighting someone else's candle. That person then shares a special word and its meaning and lights another person's candle. This continues until everyone's candle is lighted.

Invite observations about the experience.

You're now ready for the love feast. Gather everyone around a campfire or fireplace if possible. Ask everyone to find and read a scripture that contains the word "love." You might give a few hints: 1 Corinthians; 1 John 3 and 4; Romans 12; and John 13—15.

After the last scripture has been read, everyone should get up and stand beside someone and tell that person why he or she loves him or her. This may be done one at a time or all at once. Some people may wish to express love to more than one person.

This meaningful experience could be repeated on an annual basis.

LIVE LINKS

This activity is appropriate any time you want to illustrate the importance of each person as a part of the group and the body of Christ.

All you need is one box of Boomerings (from Discovery Toys) for every 12 group members. Boomerings are interconnecting links made from durable plastic. Each box contains 24 links of assorted colors. (For information about where to purchase Boomerings contact Discovery Toys, Box 232008, Pleasant Hill, CA 94523.) You can also make your own links out of paper strips.

Give each group member two links. Ask kids to hook an index finger through the links, one on each hand, then connect their links with one another's links to form a large circle. Point out that each "live link" is an important part of the "living chain," the body of Christ. Read and discuss this concept in 1 Corinthians 12:12-31.

As a closing, have each person keep one link as a reminder of his or her "belonging" to the group. Have group members each put their name on the second link. Collect these to form a chain. Display this chain in the youth group meeting room.

Use the chain in the meeting room as an object lesson for other meetings. Following are examples:

● Separate one link from the rest for a lesson on lone-

liness.
- Break the chain into three or four smaller chains for a lesson on cliques.
- Separate all the links for a discussion on individuality.

LOVE LETTERS

To give your group members a special sense of love and belonging, use this idea for your next retreat.

Before the retreat, ask group members' parents to secretly write love letters to their sons and daughters and give the letters to you or other adult volunteers. Be sure to contact all the parents and to collect letters from all the parents; you wouldn't want anyone to be left out.

At the retreat, find the right moment—

perhaps after a study on family or love—and present the letters to your young people. Give them the freedom to be alone to read their letters.

Group members receive a special dose of love, and parents will notice changed attitudes in their kids when they return.

MEATLESS DINNER

Instead of the standard staples for youth group dinners (pizza, burgers and hot dogs), why not organize a Meatless Dinner? A week before the dinner, divide into two- or three-person teams. Each team is responsible for preparing a

nutritious meatless casserole for the next week's youth dinner. Bring recipes to the dinner too.

The Meatless Dinner can be a great setting for discussions on hunger and simpler lifestyles. It can also be a part of a fund raiser for your denominational hunger programs.

MERRY-GO-ROUND MIXER

Here's a fun and interesting way to get acquainted in a group.

Form two circles, inner and outer, facing each other. Inner circle talks to outer circle with five statements, two minutes each. Shift to the right after each two-minute subject. Outer circles may ask questions but make no other comment. After five statements, repeat the same process, with the outer circle doing the talking. The leader will read the statements and call time.

Inner circle:
1. If I could visit any place in the world on vacation . . .
2. If I could smash one thing and one thing only . . .
3. If I had only one more day to live . . .
4. The time I feel most alone is . . .
5. The greatest force that has changed history . . .

Outer circle:
1. The greatest crime one person can commit against another . . .
2. The greatest discovery I'd like to make . . .
3. The greatest value in my life at the moment is . . .

4. The thing I fear the most is . . .
5. The thing that gives me the greatest satisfaction is . . .

NAIL SOUP

Have everyone bring something to put into a pot to make Nail Soup (stew). It may be meat, vegetables, mushrooms, etc. Show the movie *The Nail* from Mass Media Ministries. After the film, have your dinner of Nail Soup and talk about the movie; also tie it in with the body of Christ passages from the Bible (Romans 12:4-8), explaining that just as members each brought something for Nail Soup and made a delicious meal, so they each are a part of the body of Christ, making something special when put together.

NAME GAME

Do your group members know what their names really mean? Lead them in this discovery and understanding of the spiritual meanings of their names. You'll need a book of literal meanings of first names (some supermarkets and most bookstores have these); Bibles; and enough concordances for each person to have access to one.

Provide each member with a large sheet of colored construction paper and colored markers. Demonstrate how to draw a shield with four sections. Have each group member write his or her first name (no nicknames) in the top section of the shield.

Now read aloud, for all to hear, the literal meaning of each name, which each respective group member will write

Shield diagram:
- STEPHEN
- CROWN or GARLAND – GREEK –
- "Now there is in store for me the crown of righteousness, which the Lord, the righteous Judge, will award to me on that day—and not only to me, but also to all who have longed for his appearing." 2 Timothy 4:8
- I AM TO HELP OTHERS RECEIVE THEIR AWAITING CROWN.

in the second section of his or her shield. If a name isn't in your book, a quick call to the parents may provide the literal meaning.

Each group member now uses a Bible and concordance to find a Bible verse that conceptualizes the literal meaning of his or her name. Help group members think of alternate words if their literal-meaning words aren't listed in the concordance.

Have group members write in the third section of their shields the verses they find. And in the last section, they should write related spiritual meanings they can apply to their lives.

Close this activity by having each member show his or her shield to the group.

NEWCOMERS NIGHT

Many senior high youth groups welcome incoming freshmen with a special event at the start of school in the fall. Why not welcome them into your group at the end of the school year before, so they can join the group in summer activities?

Welcome newcomers with a special dinner in their honor. Send each graduating junior higher a personal invitation to join the senior high group members for dinner at a local restaurant. Meet together at the church first. Senior highers pay for the newcomers' meals.

If you have a large group, ask for individual group members or group officers to volunteer to sponsor new members for the dinner rather than having the whole group attend.

Use the welcoming dinner as an opportunity to distribute your summer calendar and highlight upcoming events.

Newcomers Night helps incoming members feel accepted and more comfortable with senior highers.

PARENT-KID TALK SHOW

Here's a way to spark discussion between parents and kids in a familiar setting: the talk show.

Invite parents to attend a youth group meeting. When everyone arrives, separate the parents into one group and kids into another.

Have adult volunteers take each group to a different room and give each member of each group a 3×5 card and pencil. The volunteers have everyone write on the card one question about an issue that causes problems at home. For example, "Why can't I date during the week if I come home by 11 p.m.?" or "Why do kids wear such crazy clothes?"

Have each group discuss these questions and arrive at some consensus of opinion; then choose four panelists to represent the views.

Bring everyone back together and collect the 3×5 cards. Choose a talk-show host to read questions from the 3×5 cards and address them alternately to each four-member panel.

Give each panel one minute to answer a question and then ask for questions and comments from the audience. Let panelists respond. Continue for at least two hours.

Close in prayer for better family communication.

PASS THE PEAS

Here is an unusual way to build togetherness in your group and have fun doing it.

Have the group sit in a circle. Require each group member to give his or her name and then make a distinctive statement about himself or herself. For example, "I can do four one-handed push-ups" or "I can recite the Pledge of Allegiance while standing on my head."

The participant to the right of person 1 can do one of two things. Either the participant can *doubt* person 1 or he or she can *believe* person 1. If the participant doubts person 1, then 1 must show that he or she can do the feat he or she claimed. If 1 can do it, then person 2 is required to eat a spoonful of cold peas (from a can). If 1 cannot do it, 1 is caught in his or her bluff and must eat the peas.

If person 2 chooses to believe 1, then 2 must attempt the feat—so as to prove that person 1 is not the only person in the world who can do it. If 2 accomplishes the feat, then 1 has to eat the spoonful of peas. If 2 cannot, then he or she must eat the peas.

The game continues around the circle. Now 2 makes a claim, and person 3 must be the judge.

This game often uncovers some great hidden talents in the group.

PEOPLE HUNT

Here's an adventuresome way for your group to mix with new members.

The People Hunt takes place in a busy airport, shopping mall or any other large place where many people roam.

There are two types of people in a People Hunt—the "hunted" and the "hunters." The hunters should outnumber the hunted.

One of your adult volunteers meets with the hunted (new members) at the airport. The hunted then have their pictures taken in the photo booth (or they may bring along a photo of themselves). They may disguise themselves a little—with sunglasses, a hat or whatever. Then the hunted spread out. Bathrooms are off-limits.

About a half-hour after the hunted arrive, the hunters should come as a group to the airport. Divide the hunters into groups of three and give each group a photo of the person to be hunted. When a team finds a hunted person, they exchange a coded message such as "Why didn't they play cards on the ark?" "Because Noah was sitting on the deck."

Then the hunter group finds another group of hunters and trades photos. The hunted person who was "found" joins the group and helps with the search. The hunted keep moving around to keep the hunters busy.

Allow 45 minutes for the hunt. Then everyone meets at a prearranged spot. Go out for pie and get to know the people you hunted.

This activity would also work well for an entire youth group to hunt another youth group.

PILLOW TALK

Do the members of your group feel free to express themselves? If not, maybe your problem is that the only mode of self-expression available at your group meetings is the spoken word. And we all know that words don't always get the full message across. Maybe what your group needs is the simple acquirement of some pillows.

Yes, pillows. Stock your meeting place with an abundance of multicolored, interestingly shaped, soft pillows and you'll give the less oral types just what they need to fill in the gaps that their oratory always seems to leave.

How? Like this. Let's say Lori asks Colleen how she felt

about something Lori had said. Colleen is at a loss for words. Fortunately there is a basketball-size pillow handy that, without a moment's hesitation, Colleen seizes and flings across the room where it strikes the wall. Actually, she's aiming at Lori. Then Colleen explains, "It made me kind of mad." Colleen expressed herself. And people got the message.

But pillows also help express other feelings besides anger. Does something make you happy? Toss a pillow into the air—hurray! Did something embarrass you? Bury your face in a pillow until the subject changes.

Pillows also have more practical purposes. Is the furniture in your meeting place uncomfortable? A pillow in the right place could fix that. Are there times when group members want to be closer? Don't move the furniture closer together—form a circle of pillows on the floor. And if you operate on a tight budget, good news! Pillows can be made inexpensively. There's no need to buy them ready-made. Make the pillows as a group project.

So if you want a new mode of expression that can make your group meetings more comfortable or more intimate, try pillows.

POW-WOW

This crazy activity is a good kickoff for group meetings or retreats. It allows group members to share both good and bad experiences that have happened during the week.

First, have everyone sit on the floor in a circle. Say: "We'll now have a Pow-Wow. But *this* Pow-Wow is unlike anything you've seen on television."

Explain that group members will be sharing "pow" and "wow" experiences. A "pow" is a disappointment (downer) that's occurred at home or school. A "wow" is anything that causes a smile (upper) such as a personal achievement or special recognition.

Second, find a tossable object such as an apple, pillow or shoe. Begin by sharing a "wow," and then toss the object to someone in the circle. When that person catches the object, quickly yell "wow" or "pow." The person with the object then shares a "wow" or "pow" experience. After sharing, he or she tosses the object to another person and yells "wow" or "pow." This continues until everyone in the group has shared an experience.

Close your Pow-Wow with a prayer for peace and God's support in both good and bad experiences.

PROGRESSIVE VARIATIONS

Every youth group in the whole world has had a progressive supper—a supper served in three or four courses, each at a different location (usually in homes). The group progresses from appetizer to salad to main course to dessert. They are loads of fun.

Well, here are some different twists to the traditional progressive supper:

• Travel by bicycle or any other kind of wheels (roller skates, skateboards and so on) to locations. Keep mileage down.

• Serve courses outdoors, picnic style.

• Eat each course in a different restaurant: appetizer at a health-food store (they offer a variety of juices and snacks), salad at a pizza place, main course at McDonald's and dessert at Baskin-Robbins.

• Use four different rooms in the church. Decorate them to represent four different foreign mission areas your church suggests. Serve the native foods of the areas. Brief presentations (slides, panels and talks) can explain the ministry you're seeking to provide in each area.

• Arrange American ethnic meals in homes or at the church. At each serving, dramatize the situation of each ethnic group: soul food with information on ghetto life; Polish food with a look at Polack jokes; Indian food with a discussion of the plight of America's natives; and so on. In each case the group can deal with misinformation and generalization regarding each ethnic group.

• Scripture progressive supper, in which a passage of scripture and a group experience is set up at each course, as follows:

1. Appetizer. Have the group form a circle on the lawn of the host's home. Read John 13:1-16. Explain why footwashing was a custom in a time of sandals and dirt roads and how Jesus used this task to teach his disciples about servanthood. A comparable custom in our time is the washing of hands before a meal . . . usually done alone, but this time the group members will wash one another's hands. All you need are a basin of water, a wet towel and a dry towel. While the group is doing this in silence, the scripture could be read again or the young people could sing softly.

2. Salad. Have the group form a circle on the lawn of the host's home. Read Luke 14:16-24 regarding the great banquet. Point out that Jesus has invited us to a great feast, and a lot of us still give excuses for not giving ourselves to him.

3. Main course. Have the group form a circle as before. Read Matthew 25:31-46, followed by information on world hunger. Quote Luke 12:45. Say the blessing for the entire progressive supper.

4. Dessert. Have the group form a circle. Read the scripture passage that includes Jesus telling Peter, "If you love me, feed my sheep" (John 21:4-17), followed by a modern-day parable about the man who was given a glimpse of hell and heaven. Taken to hell, he saw people sitting at a lavish banquet, but all were in great grief due to the fact that long utensils had been strapped to their arms so that their elbows could not bend. Therefore, they could not feed themselves. Then he was taken to heaven where he saw the same lavish banquet and the same utensils strapped to the people. But these people were happy, full, singing and joyous, for they were feeding the people seated across from them.

5. Then ask group members to pair off and feed each other dessert, after which the benediction is given.

THE PUZZLE

Puzzles are great starters for discussions about the unique contributions of each individual to the group.

Divide the group into groups of six to eight. Give each group 99 pieces of a 100-piece puzzle. Keep one piece from each puzzle, on which you've written a scripture reference on the back such as 1 Corinthians 12:12; Romans 12:4-5; or Ephesians 4:15-16. As each group finishes its puzzle, group members must come to you for the missing piece. Have group members discuss their scripture passages while the other groups are finishing their puzzles.

After all groups have finished, discuss the Bible passages and relate them to everyone's individual gifts and the group's need for them.

PUZZLE UNITY

To illustrate a retreat on the theme of group unity, purchase a poster and cut it into puzzle pieces (one for each member plus five extra pieces). On the bottom of the poster write "Let's Get It Together . . . Now."

Place each piece in an envelope and seal it. On the outside write "Bring to retreat." Give envelopes or send them to each retreat-bound member. Keep the five extra pieces.

At the retreat, have each person open his or her envelope and try to put the picture together. Of course, some of the pieces are missing. This leads to a discussion about how each piece contributes to the whole picture, about each member's responsibility to the group and members' unity in Christ.

Cover the puzzle with clear Con-Tact paper and hang it in your youth room at church as a reminder that the picture is not complete without each person contributing to the whole.

REGRESSIVE DINNER

The process is the same as a progressive dinner. You go to different homes for each course of the meal. The hitch here is that you do everything in reverse—start with the dessert, then move to the main course, salad and appetizer.

If you really want to have fun, have people wear their clothes backward.

ROLLER-SKATING REFLECTION NIGHT

Combine roller-skating and the topic of friendship for a memorable evening.

Rent a roller-skating rink. Divide the group into three teams, each responsible for a two-minute talk or skit on friendship and self, friendship and God or friendship and others.

After group members have been skating for 30 minutes,

have them gather together for the talk on friendship and self. Then have group members skate alone for the next 15 minutes while they reflect on how good a friend they are to themselves. Next, have the second group give its presentation on friendship and God. Give skaters 15 minutes to skate and talk with other group members about what it means to be a friend of God.

The third group then gives a talk or skit on friendship and others. Have group members select a partner to skate with for the next 15 minutes and discuss what friendship with others means to them.

Use the rest of the evening for open skating and developing friendships.

SONG SIGNS

Teaching your congregation a new song for youth Sunday? Tired of seeing the people bury their faces, and voices, in the songbook? Here's an idea to get them to look, and sing, forward.

Letter the lyrics on large pieces of posterboard. Give one poster to each kid standing in front of the congregation. As the song progresses, each poster is held up for the congregation to see and read.

This method works especially well with simple songs with few lyrics such as "Day by Day" from *Songs* (Songs and Creations).

SPAGHETTI EXTRAVAGANZA

Sponsor a successful Spaghetti Extravaganza. Everything is based on the noodle—from the meal to devotions.

Here are some activities:

● Spaghetti Dinner. Start the event with the meal. Give awards for the sloppiest eater, the biggest eater, the neatest eater. Give prizes of antacid, or a bib. (Don't serve all the noodles! Save some for what follows.)

● Pasta Pass. Have everyone draw an uncooked spaghetti noodle. Then, announce that the two people holding the shortest noodles are now team captains. They choose team members. Each member now takes a piece of uncooked spaghetti (which becomes a "pasta passer") and assembles in a line. The relay begins when the captain passes a piece of cooked spaghetti from his or her pasta passer to the next. The object is to pass the pasta down and back without using anything but the pasta passer. If a piece falls, the team must start over.

● Noodle Knots. Divide into groups of four. Each team

ties lengths of cooked spaghetti together, trying to make the longest continuous piece that can be held off the floor. Set a time limit. When time is called, the teams suspend their creations. The longest string wins. The losers eat their pieces.

● Spaghetti Toes. Divide into two teams. Take off shoes and socks. The object: to transport the most spaghetti by using the toes. Pass from person to person from a bowl to a plate at the other end. The team that transports the most in a given time is the winner.

● Javelin Throw. Pick one person from each team to throw uncooked spaghetti the longest distance.

● Spaghetti Coiffures. Each team dresses its captain with cooked spaghetti to resemble a hairdo. Arrange for pictures and judging.

● Devotions. Following a couple of songs, a lesson on spaghetti will wrap up the whole evening. Using a cooked and uncooked piece of spaghetti, point out the need for the spaghetti to jump into the boiling water to find fulfillment. The same is true of the Christian: He or she must first lose his or her life to find it (Matthew 16:25). Trials build character and confidence in God, who supplies our needs. We are transformed as we discover new potential with God.

STAFF TRIVIA

This game will appeal to your group members' love of

trivia, and also better acquaint them with the youth group adult staff—volunteers, leaders and pastor. Make sure all the adults who help with the group attend.

Begin by having group members write questions for the following four trivia categories. Following are some sample questions:

1. Sports and leisure—What's your favorite hobby?
2. Science and nature—How do you like your eggs prepared? What color best describes you in the morning?
3. Entertainment—What's your favorite TV show?
4. Arts and literature—Which of the seven dwarfs in *Snow White and the Seven Dwarfs* best describes you?

Divide the group into teams of equal numbers, and assign each team a staff member. The teams will compete to correctly answer the most questions about their staff members.

As you ask each question, the staff members must write their answers while the team members confer and then produce their best guess. Award three points for each team's correct answer; keep score.

For variety, put a few group members rather than adults on the hot seat.

SWAP LABOR FOR FUN

Ever wish you could take your group on a cruise or stay at an expensive resort? Here's a way you can make it happen. All it takes is a little research and a lot of sweat.

First, find a charter cruise service, state-owned resort or riding stable in your area.

Next, look for a project at the site requiring unskilled labor. For example, you could present the owner of a yacht charter service with a written offer to clean off the beach and paint fences for the beginning of the season. The offer could include who would furnish materials and tools, when the work would be done and what services your group would receive in return.

A project like this can lead to summer jobs for kids. Plus, it's a fun project that brings your group closer together and makes an out-of-reach activity affordable.

TALK CIRCLES

Do you want to improve your group's communication skills? Try this method and discuss the results.

Divide into groups of 10 or 12. Five or six members of each group form a small Talk Circle. The remaining members of your group surround them in an outside circle. The small Talk Circle takes on a controversial news topic or values question. For example, should abortion be outlawed? Or, should euthanasia be legalized? The members of the Talk Circle are to openly discuss the question for 10 minutes. Within that time they are to try to come to a group agreement on their answer to the question. The members of the outside group are not to participate in the discussion. Their role is to observe how well the talkers are communicating.

After 10 minutes, have both groups discuss how well the talkers listened and responded to one another. Were the outside group members able to keep silent? What can you do to improve your listening?

Repeat the experience by choosing new talkers and/or a new topic.

TINKERTOY COMMUNICATION

This exercise illustrates the importance of face-to-face, verbal communication.

Before the group meets, build a Tinkertoy structure using 20 to 25 pieces. Make sure no one sees it.

Divide the group into teams of six people. Provide each

group with Tinkertoys identical to those that you used. Each group chooses a captain, whose job is to look at the leader's structure and then send messages to his or her team on how to build an identical structure. The captain may not draw it; he or she may only describe it. Teams may send questions back to their captains at any time. Designate runners to take messages back and forth.

The winner is determined both by speed and resemblance to the original structure.

TINKERTOY TEAMS

Have some fun with tower building—and group building at the same time.

First, prepare by taking several large sets of Tinkertoys, dividing each set in half, and packaging each "half" in a large plastic bag. You'll need one bag of Tinkertoys for every six people in your group.

Now, divide the group into groups of six and give each group a bag of toys. Instruct them: "This exercise takes 10 minutes. For the first five minutes, examine the toys in your bag without removing them from the bag. Then discuss your ideas, and on paper design the tallest, strongest tower you can build with the toys. Then you will take five minutes to construct your tower—but you can't speak to each other during its construction. You may communicate in other ways, but not by talking."

After 10 minutes, call time and give each group a copy of these questions to discuss: Did you build what you designed? How did it feel to work together? What did it feel like to be a member of your team? Were you supportive of each other?

Gather all members together in one large group and ask members of each small group to explain what their tower "means" and what they discovered about themselves as they built it.

TOILET PAPER CONFESSIONS

This crazy crowdbreaker helps members get to know each other better.

Have your group sit in a circle and pass a roll of toilet paper from person to person. Instruct the young people to each take as much as they would need to blow their nose.

After everyone has taken some toilet paper, go around the circle and ask each person to tell one interesting fact about himself or herself for each square torn off.

This is great fun and everyone participates!

TRAVELING HOAGIE

Here's a new twist on the old progressive dinner idea. Instead of eating a different course at each stop along the way, you progressively build hoagies (submarine sandwiches).

Plan to travel to each member's home. At the first stop you'll get the bread and slice it. Additions at later homes could include ham, cheese, onions, oil and vinegar, lettuce and tomatos. Hoagie "accessories" could also be added—chips, salads, soft drinks and dessert.

At your last stop, you'll finally have a feast!

One word of caution: Be sure to find drivers who won't mind driving cars that'll smell like hoagies for a week.

TRIP JOURNAL

Going on a trip this summer? You will probably experience some times that will be too good to forget. So, get a volunteer or two from the group to write a Trip Journal.

At the end of each day of your trip, the journal writer should sit down and write everything that happened that day. Include good and bad things, laughs and miseries, fun and boring times. Be sure to include lots of the kids' names. It's best if you can mention each member for each day of the trip.

Write the journal like a diary—a separate entry for each

day. Don't let anyone else see your journal entries.

When you return from the trip, type the journal and have it photocopied. You may want to add some artwork on the cover, or a map showing the trail of your journey.

Then set aside a part of one of your regular youth group meetings to pass out the journals. Everybody will look forward to them with as much (or more) anticipation as the school yearbooks.

Your Trip Journal will become one of your prized possessions, read and reread year after year.

TRIP TALK

Transform those long, tiresome bus trips into productive group-building experiences. Here are several ideas to help your young people get to know each other better.

Begin by challenging each member to get to know everyone else on the bus by the end of the journey. Then have the kids arrange themselves alphabetically (by last names) two to a seat. Tell members to learn three new facts about their seat partner in addition to the person's name, and have each person introduce his or her partner to the whole bus.

Next, form groups of four by having designated pairs turn around and face another pair without changing seats. Each person in the foursome tells what he or she did the past weekend. Allow time for the four friends to visit.

Try having all group members rearrange themselves by their birthdays, still two to a seat. Again form groups of four, and have each person complete the sentence "The best birthday party I ever had was . . ." After allowing enough time for more visiting, have them complete "The best birthday present I ever received was . . ." Give kids time to visit before rearranging the group again.

Continue this process throughout your trip. Before the trip, have a committee of kids help think of other seating arrangement possibilities (for instance, shoe size, favorite color or hair color). Dream up sentence-completion possibilities that will stimulate conversation, break down barriers and create new friendships.

WE ARE THE BODY

Here's an original idea for scripture reading and a way to have total audience participation in its interpretation.

Split your group into four sections. Each is assigned a letter of the word "part," and each section is designated as a hand, foot, eye or ear.

You'll also need a reader, sign holders, a Bible, two large posters ("The Body Is One" written on one poster and "We Are . . ." written on the other) and four smaller posters with the letters P-A-R-T.

The reader begins with 1 Corinthians 12:12-26. Whenever the word "body" is read, the reader pauses, the sign holder raises the sign "The Body Is One" and everyone shouts the poster message with his or her right fist raised. The reader continues in this manner; every time a part is read, the reader pauses, the sign holders raise the letter signs, and the four sections shout the letters P-A-R-T, cheerleader style! When "eye" is read, the sign holder raises the "We Are . . ." sign and the eye section yells, "We are the eye!" as they blink their eyes. (Ear section tugs on their ears, hand section waves and foot section stomps three times.)

This well-received activity provides the body of Christ with involvement and participation in this scripture reading.

WHITE SHIRT PARTY

Here's a creative activity to help your members get to know one another better. It also works well in a retreat setting where several groups gather together.

Round up old white dress shirts for everyone. You'll find them in your rag bags at home or at the Salvation Army and

Goodwill stores. And you'll need a permanent ink felt-tip marker for each person. Spread some papers on the floor to protect it from the ink that may seep through the shirts.

Give these instructions to each person:

1. Write your first name on the front left pocket.
2. Write your last name under the back of the shirt.
3. On the back, write your favorite color and your height in centimeters.
4. Write your birthday.
5. Draw an animal you would like to be.
6. Answer: Why are you here?

7. Draw an eye the color of yours.
8. Identify your favorite musical instrument.
9. Draw a flower you like.
10. Write a nursery rhyme title.
11. List your hobbies.
12. Identify your favorite sport.
13. Write your favorite saying (words you like, a proverb, some philosophy or a Bible verse).
14. Draw your favorite fruit.
15. Answer: What do you need to improve in yourself?
16. Identify a food you dislike.
17. Draw something that you like to do in the winter.
18. Draw your favorite possession.

When everyone is finished, each person should put on his or her shirt. Now continue with a mixer or your planned program for the evening. This is an easy and effective way to get acquainted. Suddenly all the people in the room are wearing their personalities where everyone can see them.

WHO IS THE VISITOR?

Welcome youth group visitors by playing a game to guess each visitor's full name. Here's how it works.

Break your group into as many groups as there are letters in the visitor's name. For example, if Jo Nelson is the visitor, there should be eight small groups. Give each small group one letter from the name to act out without talking. Suggest pantomiming a biblical character, idea or event that begins with that same letter.

So, for Jo Nelson, group 1 might act out Jesus washing his disciples' feet. Once the whole group guesses the correct answer, "Jesus," everyone knows the visitor's first name starts with "J." Group 2 might act out a scene that portrays "obedience" to God, and group 3 might pose as the "Nativity" scene.

Jesus, obedience and Nativity correspond to the first three letters of Jo's name. Ask those who know the visitor's name not to tell.

This game is so enjoyable that group members may actively recruit visitors.

WHOSE SECRET IS IT?

Everyone likes secrets. Especially if it's okay to share them with someone else. And that's the object of this crowdbreaker.

Have youth group members each write on a 3×5 card something no one else in the group knows about them. For example, "I won a perfect attendance certificate in the second-grade" or "My favorite sandwich is bananas and pickles." Put all the secrets in a hat.

Each person then picks out a secret from the hat. On "go," group members go from person to person to find out who wrote the secret they chose. The person whose secret it is must sign the 3×5 card. The first three people to find the writer of their secret are the winners.

When everyone is done, have the group sit on the floor. Then have each person read the secret he or she chose and identify the person who wrote it.

For fun, the whole activity could be done in whispers!

YARN CIRCLE

Unity and cooperation are vital ingredients in any successful group. These qualities can be graphically demonstrated in a Yarn Circle.

Have everyone stand in a circle. Someone begins by mentioning something he or she is thankful for. He or she then tosses a ball of yarn to another person in the circle, being careful to hang on to the end of the yarn. The recipient of the ball of yarn then mentions something he or she is thankful for, and tosses it to another person, holding on to his or her bit of yarn. This goes on until everyone has had a chance to contribute at least once. By this time, the yarn should have created an intricate pattern, interweaving all of your members.

Then, slowly, a few of the members should drop their sections of yarn, making the pattern sag. In order to take up the slack, all remaining members of the circle must back up. Repeat this a couple of times.

Then everyone should have a chance to reflect on what just occurred. Mention that the beautiful pattern was possible only with everyone's involvement. And when some members dropped out, the yarn design became ugly and the group was ultimately forced to grow farther apart.

This is a good exercise to repeat periodically.

Growing In

100 PERCENT CHANCE OF RAIN

This setting-priorities exercise works well with both junior highers and senior highers.

The publicity reads: "Imagine you are Noah. You know it's going to rain for 40 days and 40 nights. You also know that dams will burst, rivers will overflow, sewers will back up—the Earth will be covered with water. God tells you that he'll permit only you and a few others to board the Royal Princess.

"Space is a major restriction on the Royal Princess. You may bring along only what you can carry in your arms.

"What will you bring with you? Think about it this week. Bring those items to the meeting (give date, place and time).

"We'll talk about what we brought with us and why. If you can't bring something, like a water bed, bring a picture or a drawing of the item."

The variety of items kids bring to this meeting is always wide: stuffed and real animals, stereos, a baby sister. This activity prompts enthusiastic discussion about priorities and the end of the world.

AMERICANS AND FOREIGNERS

For an interesting look at the American lifestyle we often take for granted, use this discussion starter.

Divide the group into small groups of four to six and choose one person from each group to be the American. Then have everyone else, the foreigners, give all of their purses, wallets, watches and jewelry to the American in their group.

Tell the Americans that they now own all of the possessions that belonged to the families of the foreigners. Tell the foreigners that all of them and their families now live together and must share all the possessions and food that were meant for only one family. Paint a picture that group members can relate to; tailor the tale of poverty to conditions in your own area.

Give group members time to think about and discuss what living like this would be like. Ask: "How does it feel to be rich/poor? How does it feel to know that others are rich/poor? Has this affected your relationship with God in any way?"

Use Matthew 25:31-46 for discussion afterward.

APPRECIATION ADJECTIVES

Here's a short and sweet activity to help your group members feel closer to one another.

Have everyone sit together in a circle. Tell group members to look around the circle and quietly think of a positive one-word description for each person. Then have kids, one by one, look at every other person and slowly say the names and adjectives in this way: "Casey is thoughtful; Mark is funny . . ."

Group members will feel better for having taken the time to give and receive warm thoughts that otherwise may remain unsaid.

BALLOON CONFESSIONS

We often overlook the Christian practice of confession of sins. Here's an experience to bring meaning to the act of confession and forgiveness.

You'll need one helium balloon for each person in your group. And you'll need a batch of felt-tip markers. Each person writes on the balloon a sin that he or she wishes to confess.

Then the group goes outside and offers a prayer for forgiveness. And each person silently talks to God about his or her sins and then releases the balloon, symbolic of God's forgiveness.

BALLOON PUTDOWNS

Decrease putdowns and increase compliments with the following activity.

Give a balloon and string to each young person as he or she enters the meeting room. Have the members blow up the balloons and tie them to their right ankles. Start the game: Instruct everyone to stomp on each other's balloons until they are all popped. Tell the young people to remember their feelings when their balloons are popped and when they pop others' balloons.

Then have members form small groups of three and discuss feelings. Ask: "How do you feel when your ego-balloon is popped at home? school? by your best friend? at youth group meeting?"

Form a circle and give each person a pencil and paper. Instruct each person to sign his or her name at the top of

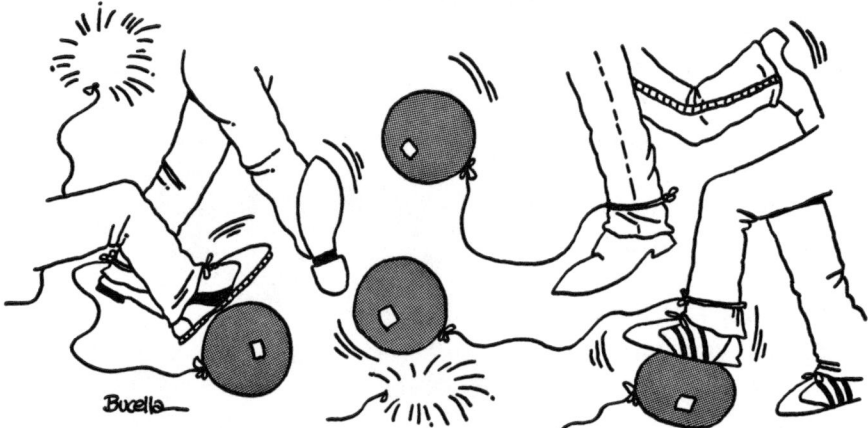

the page and pass it to the right. Pass the papers around the circle; ask the group members to write positive statements about each person on the appropriate paper. Continue until each person receives his or her paper back.

Compare the affirming statements to putdowns. Ask: "How do each of these types of statements make you feel? How does God want us to treat others? What are some ways to do that?"

Close by reading John 13:34. Pray for God's help as you build up others in the world.

BIBLE STUDY SCAVENGER

Here's a way to add a little action and a lot of objects to your Bible study. This activity combines a Bible study, a scavenger hunt and a show-and-tell session.

This unusual study begins after you've completed your

planned Bible study. Break into teams and divide the passages you just studied among the teams. (The Gospels and Old Testament stories work best, but any passage is okay if you think hard enough.)

Now, using the passage as a guide, list any item that's mentioned or implied in the passage. You'll have to use your imagination as you reread the verse. Some possible objects aren't always immediately obvious in the verses.

For instance, potential items from Mark 2:13-17 might include water from the lake (verse 13); dusty footprints from the crowd (verse 13); a tax receipt from the tax collector's booth (verse 14); hamburger wrappers from the dinner with the tax collectors and sinners (verse 15); certificates of achievement for the Pharisees who were lawyers (verse 16); and a doctor's bill for the sick sinners (verse 17).

Once each team has listed all the items in its passage, take an hour or so and scavenge the items from around the church or neighborhood. At the end of the time limit, one person on the team reads the passage slowly while the remaining team members illustrate it with the items.

After the scavenged study is over, you can use the items in a "museum." Pick up some small tags from a business supply store or use 3×5 cards. Describe the item museum-style and list the Bible verse that mentions it.

Set up a creative display in an out-of-the-way area of the church and take church school classes on tours.

BIBLE TREASURE HUNT

This game is especially suited for a youth retreat or some other setting in which there is plenty of room. It is best played outdoors.

Before the game, select a Bible verse, one that is fairly well known to your group, but one that no one will think of immediately. Write each word of the verse on a separate piece of paper, and hide the pieces of paper in various locations around the play area. Compose a set of clues, in duplicate, that will direct the players to each one of the hidden words. Unlike an ordinary treasure hunt, the clues do not form a chain; each clue directs the players to a separate hidden word.

Now divide your group into two teams. Give each team a complete set of clues. The two teams (which each have an identical set of clues) will compete to find a single set of hidden words. Most likely, each team will end up with roughly half of the hidden words of the Bible verse. Once each team finds as many of the words as it can, it gathers at a previously designated location to try to unscramble the Bible verse.

Now the real fun begins. In all likelihood, neither team will have found enough of the words to figure out the verse. At this point, permit the teams to bargain with one another, trading one word for another until one of the teams wins by figuring out the Bible verse.

The key to winning this game is organization and cooperation. The teams are competing with each other for the same set of hidden words; therefore, the team that first sits down and brainstorms about the clues, then delegates certain team members to go out and retrieve the words, will do much better than the team that immediately runs out helter-skelter. A wide range of abilities is essential—not just speed in running, but also skill in problem-solving, verbal ability and familiarity with the Bible. Thus, all team members can feel that they played a part.

THE BODY

Read (or study) 1 Corinthians 12:12-26 to the group. Take a few minutes to discuss Paul's vision of Christians in community as the body of Christ. As a body, all members affect and support the others—if the head aches the whole body suffers; if the eyes are closed the whole body stumbles; and if the feet hurt the body won't get so far.

Pass out pieces of paper and have each person write the part of the body he or she thinks he or she represents, and why. For example, Joe is the smile, because he keeps us

happy; Amy is the hand, because she works hard; and so on. Then have each person share his or her "part of the body." (This works well as a get-acquainted exercise too.)

Celebrate the diversity and the interdependence of the parts with a song or prayer together to affirm Christ's presence in your group.

BODY PARTS

Here's a good discussion starter for devotions on 1 Corinthians 12:12-31.

Cover an open doorway with butcher paper. In the center, cut a hole that is 3 inches in diameter.

Divide the group into teams of three or four. Send one team at a time behind the door. Tell the team members to, one at a time, each place a different body part up to the hole. Instruct the other teams to write what each part is, and who they think it belongs to (for example, Sally's ear, Joe's elbow or Pete's tongue).

Your group members will discover how hard it is to pick out a person by one part. Emphasize that this is how it is with the body of Christ: We are all parts in that body, but it is hard to be recognized as a witness in the world if only one part (person) is being seen.

A discussion of 1 Corinthians 12:12-31 after this game will complete the lesson.

BOOKS FOR A SECRET FRIEND

This activity encourages unity in a group. It also works well in a retreat setting.

You'll need a basket, colored paper, pens, pencils, markers, crayons, magazines, scissors, staplers, glue and tape.

Gather group members together. Have everyone (including leaders) write his or her name on a piece of paper and place it in a basket. Everyone draws a name and becomes that person's secret friend for the duration of the event. Remind everyone to keep the name secret until the closing service.

Explain that each person is to make a booklet using pictures, drawings, poems, etc. The booklet reflects positive qualities such as talent, character and personality traits each person sees in his or her secret friend.

Show the booklets, reveal the secret friend's name and describe the booklet's contents one at a time during the closing prayer service. End with a group hug and familiar song.

CASSETTE TAPE RECORDER PARABLES

Try this simple idea: Choose a parable and think of the sounds that accompany it. Then record the parable—with the sound effects, of course.

The methods are varied:

● Create a recording to present to group members during a study of a particular passage.

● Let small groups of members choose different parables and spend 45 minutes working on recordings to present to the whole youth group.

● Have all group members work together to produce sound effects and record a parable to present to the congregation.

Whatever the method, imagination is important. If your passage says, "And when he comes home," record the stomp-stomp-stomping of footsteps and the sounds of opening and closing a door. Improvise. If the passage talks about sheep, record a chorus of young people "b-a-a-ing."

And when your "work" is done, sit back, relax and listen—really listen—to the Bible passages.

CHRISTMAS DEVOTION

Here's an activity to help kids anticipate the Christmas season.

Ask group members how they would complete the sentence "Christmas is . . ." Give everyone a minute to write or think of a reply. At the count of three, have everyone simultaneously shout his or her sentence.

Explain: "That was difficult to understand, wasn't it? Sometimes the message of Christmas gets lost in the noise and celebration. We have to be quiet and listen to Jesus to get the real meaning of Christmas."

One at a time, ask each person to share how he or she completed the sentence "Christmas is . . ."

Give each person an unlighted candle and have the group members sit in a circle in silence. Light the candles from one person to the next. When all candles are lighted, sing "Silent Night."

CHRISTMAS "GIFT LIST" EXCHANGE

For a meaningful, inexpensive gift exchange among youth group members this year, try this one.

Have everyone sit together in a circle. Tell group members to think of what Christmas present they'd give to each person in the group if the cost didn't matter. Encourage kids to choose personal gifts, based on their friends' interests and needs. For example, someone might give a friend a scholarship to a particular college, a year of no fights with a sister or a giant chocolate bar. Tell members that "the sky is the limit," but no unkind gifts are allowed.

Give each person a piece of construction paper and a colored marker. Tell group members each to decorate their paper to look like a gift box and put their name at the top. Have group members then pass their "boxes" to the person on their right. Tell them to write on the paper their gift to the person whose name appears at the top. Then, the gift-givers each sign their names next to their gifts. Continue this until everyone has his or her own paper back.

Allow the kids a few moments to read their papers silently. Then, let volunteers read aloud their gift lists. The gift-givers may tell why they chose the gifts for each person.

Close with a brief devotional on how God's gift to us (John 3:16) is the most personal gift we could ever receive.

CLONE PARTY

Use this backdoor approach to emphasize each youth group member's special uniqueness: Have a Clone Party!

When you publicize the party, distribute a list of requirements for attendance: Everyone must wear non-signature blue jeans, a white shirt, a white sock on the left foot and a black one on the right, tennis shoes and no jewelry; everyone must chew gum; and so on.

Tailor games to the "everyone do the same thing the same way" idea.

At snack time, instruct your "clones" to eat using their left hands only.

At some point, have group members get into small groups and list things they have in common (for example, use the same brand of toothpaste; play the same sport; like the same type of music; and shower in the morning).

Then as a whole group, discuss the lists and why they are so short. Emphasize that no matter how much we try to conform, we can't escape the fact that God created each of us *differently*.

Close your Clone Party with a devotion from 1 Corinthians 12 about how each person is unique and special in God's eyes.

COOKIE DECORATORS

A simple sugar cookie recipe is needed plus some imagination to put together an experience that provides a built-in snack and sharing session for your group.

Give each person a small amount of cookie dough and ask each person to make one or two cookies that represent something important in his or her life. Food coloring and "extras" (such as decorating candies) may be added to make the cookies come to life. It doesn't take long to bake the cookies in the oven (10-15 minutes).

Once all are finished, put them on display and ask each member of the group to tell why he or she made the kind of cookie he or she did. After the sharing of ideas, share the cookies!

CUSTOM DEVOTIONALS

It's hard for many of us to set aside a devotional time each day. And good devotional guides are hard to find. So, solve the problem by writing your own. Kids like to get involved and share the homemade guides with their friends. The friends are interested because the booklets are written by people they know. Each member selects a favorite Bible verse and then writes what it means to him or her. The youth pastor then writes a thought and challenge for the day.

Here's a sample page from a booklet:

> "God has said, 'Never will I leave you; never will I forsake you.' So we say with confidence, 'The Lord is my helper; I will not be afraid. What can man do to me?' " (Hebrews 13:5b-6).
>
> This verse has meant a lot to me since I moved to Arcadia because I had to change schools right in the middle of the year. For some reason, I'm afraid of school and I, like most others, despise going back after vacation.
>
> But Jesus helped me to meet a lot of Christian friends at school and I'm learning that school is nothing to be afraid of.
>
> There are so many verses that talk about not being afraid. Just think of what this verse says about fear.
>
> Thought: Is there anything that scares you about school and friends? What about your future? What scares you today? Trust God right now to give you peace and to help you deal with things you fear.

DECISION-MAKING

Everyone makes decisions daily. Obviously, some are more important than others. Some are so important that they require thought, study, investigation and prayer before a decision is made. These decisions may include buying a car, getting married and changing jobs. Some decisions, like whether to drink tomato juice or orange juice for breakfast, require little thought. They are "automatic," and we make many of those kinds of decisions every day. It is important to know which decisions require deliberation; different people will have different answers.

On the following form are 10 typical decisions. On the lines below these, have members list 10 more decisions that they have made during the last week or month. Try to include decisions from each of the following categories: personal and social decisions; health and safety decisions; educational and career decisions; moral, ethical and spiritual decisions; and common, everyday decisions.

After everyone has filled in the form, discuss your decision-making processes. Where do you agree and disagree? How should you establish your decision-making process? Should you consult God before every decision? Should decisions about your faith in God be automatic, or should they be carefully studied?

Decision-Making

On the lines labeled "Rank," write in a number from 0 to 5, using this scale:
- 0—not generally perceived as being under your control; decision usually is made by others.
- 1—automatic or routine; never think about it before deciding.
- 2—occasionally think about it before deciding.
- 3—think about it but don't study it or investigate it.
- 4—study and think about it a little; ask others about it a little; ask others about it before deciding; pray about it.
- 5—study and think about it a lot; ask questions; read about it before deciding; pray about it a lot.

Decision	Rank
1. To get up in the morning	_____
2. To decide what to eat and when	_____
3. To tell the truth	_____
4. To criticize a friend behind his or her back	_____
5. To change jobs	_____
6. To stop at stop signs	_____
7. To drive beyond the speed limit	_____
8. To believe in God	_____
9. To decide what classes to take	_____
10. To do homework	_____
11. _____	_____
12. _____	_____
13. _____	_____
14. _____	_____
15. _____	_____
16. _____	_____
17. _____	_____
18. _____	_____
19. _____	_____
20. _____	_____

Permission to photocopy this handout granted for local church use only. Copyright © 1988 by Group Books, Inc., Box 481, Loveland, CO 80539.

DESIGNER JEANS

Here's a fun way to use a fashion idea to show your appreciation for others' unique gifts.

Draw a large jean pocket on an 8½ ×11 piece of paper. Give each young person a photocopy of a pocket. Tell each member to write his or her name on the label and then describe, on the pocket, the kind of person that would wear these jeans (emphasizing what the wearer does or feels). For example, Mary Jones Jeans. The kind of person who wears Mary Jones Jeans likes summer more than winter, has long talks with old friends and watches the sunrise alone.

Afterward, each person shares his or her Designer Jeans description. Note that all have identified themselves in a positive way. Read Psalm 139 (especially verse 14) and thank God for the "wonder of you."

FAME

Here's an activity sure to generate discussion on fame and the definition of real "importance."

Begin by providing newsprint, colored construction paper, ribbon, markers and tape. Instruct group members to create a "fame costume" for one member of the group.

When they've finished making one member "famous," ask group members to discuss the significance of the costume. Why did they decorate the famous member of the group as they did?

Ask: "Who are some famous people you've met? Who are some famous people you'd like to get to know? Why? What qualities do you think they have that you want?"

Put pictures of 10 famous people on the wall and ask group members to rank them in order of most to least famous. Have members list on newsprint or on the fame costume the elements of fame they used to make their decisions.

Add another picture: one of Jesus. Put it right up there next to the president. Discuss ways in which elements of fame fit Jesus. Ask: "How would the media treat Jesus today? Would he be famous? Why or why not?"

Mention that although Jesus may not be a famous person from the world's point of view, he is the greatest person we can ever meet. Close with a brief discussion on God's view of importance.

FOOD FOR FOOD

Here's an idea for spicing up retreat mealtimes and meeting snack breaks, while emphasizing Bible memorization.

At retreats, give young people and adults "mental attitude builders" (Bible verses) to memorize. Some examples of positive verses are Isaiah 41:10; Philippians 2:13; Philippians 4:8; and 2 Timothy 1:7. Let members know they'll be required to quote one verse per meal before they can eat.

At each meal, assign a "judge" (a kid or an adult) to stand toward the front of the line. Only those people who correctly quote the verse can get food. Anyone who fails goes back to the end of the line.

Use this same idea during regular meeting times. Give group members a Bible verse to memorize during the week. Then at the next meeting, a group member gets refreshments only after he or she correctly quotes the verse.

FOOTWASHING

Here's a memorable Easter idea.

First, contact five youth group members who feel confident sharing in front of other people. Assign each of them one of these objects: a crown of thorns, a goblet, a small leather bag spilling coins, a pair of leather sandals and a loaf of bread. Tell the group members that they'll share what Easter means to them, using the objects.

For the meeting, set six chairs in front of the group. Next to the chair farthest to the right, place a large empty basin and a pitcher filled with water.

As the meeting begins, sit in the chair farthest to the right. Each of the young people you asked to help with this part of the meeting comes forward, explains the significance of his or her object, shares what Easter means to him or her, and sits in one of the chairs, beginning on the left.

After each person has shared, have a group member read John 13:1-17. As he or she reads, stand up and wrap a large beach towel around your pants or skirt. Slowly pour water into the basin, and take it to the group member seated on the far left. After the group member silently removes his or her shoes and socks, wash and dry the person's feet.

After you finish washing the fifth person's feet, silently set the basin and pitcher aside and have the group gather its chairs into a circle. You may want to let group members wash each other's feet voluntarily.

Take communion together. Close the meeting with a simple prayer, then remain silent to allow the young people to think about the meeting's message as they leave.

FORGIVENESS TEST

This activity is designed to help group members examine their attitudes about forgiveness in relation to the behavior of others.

Write the following situations on a chalkboard:
1. Mrs. Jones steals food for her hungry family.
2. Billy steals 50 cents from his father's wallet.
3. Fifteen-year-old Rita shoplifts with a group of friends for fun.
4. Bartender Louie goes looting during a riot in the inner city.
5. Judy requisitions small articles from the place where she works and takes them home for her personal use.
6. Jimmy snatches a purse from an old lady who has just cashed her welfare check.
7. Mary steals money from a wealthy home where she is babysitting.
8. Nancy pads her expense account.
9. Mike steals drugs to support his habit.
10. Once again Perry steals your time—promises to meet you for lunch and doesn't show up.

Now, have everyone choose the three people he or she is most willing to forgive. Then ask members to choose the three they are least willing to forgive.

Then have kids find a partner and talk about the following: why you made the choices you did; the person on the chalkboard who bothers you the most; and how God might see some of these situations.

FRIENDS DURING THE WEEK

This creative communication aid works during the week rather than at the youth meeting itself.

At a meeting, distribute 3×5 cards and ask each person to write his or her name and phone number. Notice which group members aren't present and fill out cards for them also.

Put all cards in a basket and have each member pick one.

Deliver cards to members who aren't present and "fill them in" on what's happening.

Challenge your young people to be special friends during the week to the person whose name they picked. They could send notes of encouragement and appreciation; they could each telephone their person to see if there are any prayer needs; or they could each leave little friendship packages—cookies, messages or whatever—in their person's school locker. The possibilities are limitless.

Group members will get to know each other better. And as more friendships develop outside of the church environment, your group will realize a stronger unity when all members are together.

A variation of this activity is to draw names, then keep each other's identity secret. For one week, secret friends can write affirming anonymous notes. At the end of the week, have a Name-That-Secret-Friend Party. Let everyone try to guess his or her secret friend. Reveal the identities during the party.

GIFT LIST

Here's an activity to help your group members recognize and value the gifts God has given them.

Hand out blank sheets of paper, and have each participant number down the page from 1 to 10. Have members list the gifts they have—the things they do well. Then have them look over their lists and place a star beside the gifts they really enjoy using.

Now, gather in groups of four to share lists. In the groups, focus on one person at a time, helping that person identify the gifts and abilities he or she might have missed.

Tell kids to spend a few moments considering their abilities and how they might use them to help others.

Now, gather in groups of four to share lists. In the groups, focus on one person at a time, helping that person identify the gifts and abilities he or she might have missed.

Tell kids to spend a few moments considering their abilities and how they might use them to help others.

Now divide the foursomes into pairs. Members each choose one or two of their gifts and help one another think of ways these gifts can be of value to others.

Gather the whole group together and ask members to

think about the lists they made.

Ask: "Was it difficult to identify your gifts? Why or why not? Were you surprised to discover you could list so many or so few? Explain."

Ask people to share what they learned during the experience.

GRAB BAG INSIGHTS

Encourage your young people to reflect on their own lives with this creative activity.

Fill a bag with a variety of items such as an orange, a small bottle of water, an old magazine, candy, gum, an old shoe, two pennies in a tiny bag, a note saying "I love you" and a Christmas card. Make sure there is at least one item for each group member.

Have everyone sit together in a circle. Have an adult play background music, either from another room or a hidden area of the same room. Pass the bag around. Tell group members that when the music stops, whoever has the bag must choose one item and show it to the group. That person then must complete the sentence "This item is like or unlike me because . . ." Let group members keep the items they choose—at least until the game is over.

Continue until each member has had a chance to choose from the bag or until your time is up.

GRADUATES BANQUET

Near the time of graduation, invite all members of the senior class to a dinner in their honor in your parish hall.

Invite the parents too. The dinner is a potluck affair provided by the parents and members of the junior class in the parish.

This affair is not one last attempt at religion but rather an evening of fun and celebration. Invite the seniors' parents to provide a baby picture of their child. Collect these in advance and develop a sketch of each senior. Have the juniors write a short prophecy about each senior and select some song—pop, contemporary, golden oldie or whatever—that suggests in some way the particular senior. At the banquet, have everyone try to guess the seniors. First play the song to begin the guessing process. Then read the prophecy. Finally, project the baby picture.

To end the program read the senior class will, but do it "a la Howard Hughes." Have the seniors write their own will, but unbeknown to them, the juniors also write one for the seniors. This provides much merriment.

HEAVENLY PASS

Here's a thought-provoking exercise that can lead into an interesting discussion.

Hand out 5×8 cards and pencils to the group members.

Have each person write a "pass" that might get him or her into heaven. The pass is an answer to the question, "If you were to die tonight, why should God let you into heaven?" Collect the cards and read some of them to the group. Then use the following questions for discussion:

1. How do you think someone who has never heard of Jesus Christ would answer the question?

2. Do you think someone who has never heard the gospel will be judged differently than someone who has? If so, what do you think the criteria for judgment might be? (Read Romans 1:20-21.)

3. Will our good works help us in any way when we face judgment? If so, in what way?

4. Is it possible for a person to know for certain that he or she will be admitted into heaven when he or she dies? Explain.

IF I COULD

Here's a successful group-sharing idea. Have everyone write his or her name on a 3×5 card, fold it and drop it in a box. After stirring the cards, have each person draw one from the box (or pick another if his or her own name is drawn). Then, everyone reads the name on the card, gives that person an If I Could gift and tells why.

This activity can be a serious time or a fun time of gag gifts. Some kids may give cars, new boyfriends or girlfriends, jobs, talents, success, love or friendship. You'll have a good time and a lot of participation with this simple activity.

LET GOD'S LIGHT SHINE

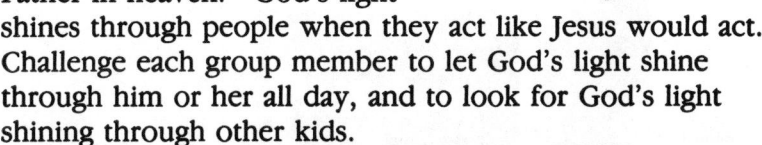

Boost your group members' self-esteem with this shining object lesson that lasts all day. This works great on a retreat or trip.

Begin the day with a devotional from Matthew 5:16: "Let your light shine before men, that they may see your good deeds and praise your Father in heaven." God's light shines through people when they act like Jesus would act. Challenge each group member to let God's light shine through him or her all day, and to look for God's light shining through other kids.

At the end of the day, give each kid a small brown paper bag with scissors, a pen and a quarter inside. Ask the kids to remember how they saw God's light shine through each group member that day. Have kids use the quarter as a pattern to cut a circle for each other group member out of the bag. On one side of each circle, have kids write one group member's name. On the other side of the circle, have kids write how God's light shone through that person that day.

Then have kids, one at a time, each place their cut-up bag over a votive candle. As the candlelight shines through the holes, have other kids tell how they saw God's light shine through that person.

When everyone has had a turn, have kids give their paper-bag circles to the group members whose names are on them.

LIGHT IN THE DARKNESS

Here's a bright idea for a rainy day.

Arrive at your group's meeting room early and set a candle in a place where it can be seen but not easily noticed. Light the candle.

When the group members arrive, read together John 1:6-13 and discuss possible reasons why people don't pay attention to Jesus. Have the group list the ideas.

After a few minutes of the discussing and listing, quietly turn off the lights. Then encourage group members to think why they didn't realize the candle was in the room. Compare their thoughts with the ideas on the list.

Close your discussion with the challenge of Matthew 5:16.

LIVING WATER

This is a fun and meaningful learning experience.

Ask everyone to bring any kind of container that holds a liquid. Any size or shape is okay but should include a lid. Each person then lists the ways he or she uses water in a week's time.

Then everyone hikes to an unknown destination selected by a leader. Here everyone fills his or her container from a creek, well or other water source.

Ask someone to read the scripture of Jesus and "living water" (John 4:5-14). Using a large poster, list the ways we are all different (like the containers) but can still have living water within us. Then list the ways living water can be used through us.

Use the containers of water at home during the following week to water plants as a reminder of physical service.

THE LOST COIN

Use this Bible study idea to illustrate the parable of the lost coin (Luke 15:8-10) and God's concern for us.

Place a handful of pennies in a small cardboard box or a large bowl. Drop in one nickel with the pennies.

Blindfold group members one at a time. Time the number of seconds it takes each person to retrieve the "lost coin" from the pennies. Have the person who just "found" the nickel hide it for the next searcher.

A shiny penny mounted on a small block of wood makes a great prize for the person with the fastest time.

Other related Bible studies are Matthew 13:44-46, dealing with the kingdom of God; and Mark 12:41-44, about the widow's offering and how Jesus embraces a good heart.

LOVE LINE

Use letter writing to build closer, more meaningful relationships.

You need a clothesline and clothespins. Give group members each a clothespin and have them write their name on it. String the line where it's easily accessible, and place the clothespins on it.

Have the group members write to each other notes of love, appreciation and/or encouragement. Stress that the notes should be positive; no putdowns allowed. Group members may write the notes on a special night or over a long period of time. Clip notes to the individuals' pins. Writers may include their names or leave notes unsigned.

Make sure everyone receives notes; recruit members to write to those who receive few.

Your whole group will discover the thrill of spreading and receiving words of love and thanks.

LOVE RAFFLE

Here's a raffle where nobody is the loser.

For your next gathering of lots of kids, pass out name tags that each have a number. Then have your raffle, drawing several numbers from the hat.

The prize? It's "the love of the brethren"! Have the winners come to the front of the room. Then encourage everyone to come and express their love to the winners—hugs, handshakes and hellos.

Even if you use this several times, winners feel special and never forget the experience.

If you wish, you can "rig" the winning numbers to be sure to include those shy, depressed or unknown people who really *need* the experience.

MARTHA-WORRIES BAG

Here's a good idea for a morning prayer service at a retreat.

Read the story of Martha and Mary (Luke 10:38-42). Introduce a large brown bag with the words "Martha-Worries Bag" written on it. Explain that Jesus had something special to share with Martha and Mary, but Martha was too busy worrying to pay attention. Say: "In the same way, Jesus has something special to share with us today. And we want to share with each other."

Invite group members to get in touch with what's bothering them such as worries about homework, problems at home or worries about a fellow group member. Have them write these worries on a 3×5 card.

Collect all the "worry cards" and put them in the Martha-Worries Bag. As you set the bag aside for the rest of the weekend, ask group members to mentally set their worries aside. You could also place the Martha-Worries Bag on a little altar as a symbol of group members offering their problems to God.

MEETING IN THE DARK

Here's a meeting idea to illustrate Jesus as the light of the world.

Have your regular program in the dark. Start with songs, a game, announcements and refreshments (popcorn). End with a devotion.

To start the devotion, light a

small candle. After about 45 minutes in the dark, the light should be a relief to the group. Ask members to survey the chaos around them (especially with the popcorn). How was the darkness? Was it easy to work together? Who got refreshments and who didn't? Did members trust each other in the dark? Compare the candlelight to Christ's light in a confused world.

Pass out candles to everyone. Then pass the light around.

ME METER

Plan an entire meeting where everybody is forbidden to say "I," "me," "myself" or any other reference to self.

At the beginning of the meeting, give each member a photocopied paper strip like the one shown. This Me Meter

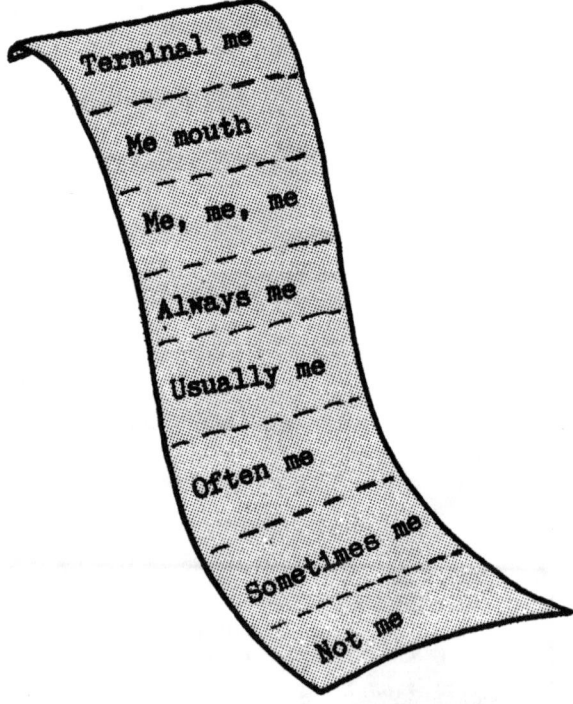

should be pinned on the front of each person. Then proceed with your meeting—mixer, discussion, refreshments, etc. Each time a member refers to himself or herself, the nearest person to him or her tears off the bottom section of the violator's Me Meter.

See who has the shortest and the longest Me Meters at the end of the meeting. The very experience of trying to speak without mentioning yourself is eye-opening and thought-provoking. Members may think twice the next time they're tempted to talk about themselves or offer their own criticism, opinion or complaint to a situation that would benefit from their silence.

You may want to reserve a period of time at the end of the meeting for a discussion of how we often dominate our speech with references to ourselves.

For brave and ambitious groups, plan an entire weekend retreat where "I" and "me" are forbidden.

MORE HAMBURGER THAN STEAK

This is a fun exercise to help everyone get acquainted.

Ask participants to think whether they are more to one extreme than the other. For example, ask, "Are you more hamburger than steak?" Those who are more like steak go to the opposite side of the room. Participants pair off and discuss briefly why they are more hamburger or steak.

Repeat the exercise by naming other extremes.

Here's a list to use: country/city, television/books, leader/follower, pioneer/settler, giver/receiver, breakfast/dinner, spectator/participant, early riser/late-nighter, mountains/beach, tiger/kitty cat, clown/straight man, country-western/classical, Cadillac/Datsun and spender/saver.

MULTIPLYING MONEY

According to Matthew 25:14-30, three servants were given sums of money by their master. The master left on a trip. When he returned, two of the servants reported they had invested the money and multiplied it for their master. But the third servant had buried the money he had been given. This servant told his master that he was afraid the master would rob him of the profit he earned, so he hid the money until the master's return. The master was angry and told the servant he could have at least put the money in the bank where it would have earned interest.

At one church, instead of the offering being collected one Sunday, the plate was passed around full of dollar bills with the invitation to take one. More than 300 dollar bills were taken and were put to work by members of the congregation. They gathered in the church parking lot one Sunday to sell items they had made and grown.

Many types of goods were sold. There were macramé owls, wall hangings, pot hangers, edible painted pies, homemade bread, plaques, paintings, jewelry, flowers, homemade noodles and fresh garden vegetables. Personal services also were provided such as babysitting, window washing and lawn care.

The proceeds gathered went to feed the hungry of the world.

This same idea would work just as well with just the youth group. The $1 is bound to grow unless it's buried in the ground.

THE NEW ME

New Year's offers a convenient opportunity to see where we have been and where Christ's unlimited power to change us may lead. The New Me is a learning experience that celebrates God's work through us and sets goals for his work in us for the coming year.

Gather pieces of posterboard (at least 14 inches × 17 inches), sheets of paper, writing utensils, creative materials (cotton balls, construction paper, markers, toothpicks), a Bible and glue. You'll also need an instant-print camera and film (or photos of each member brought from home).

Photograph each person as he or she arrives. Pass out the paper, posterboard and writing utensils. Instruct members to do the following:

1. List up to 10 good changes you've seen in yourself within the last year. Then list up to 10 concerns or problems you're struggling with. Share these lists in pairs or trios. Then read 2 Corinthians 5:17 and Colossians 3:1-4. Discuss briefly how you've seen Christ change people.

2. Write 10 goals for yourself for the coming year. Narrow this to the five most realistic ones. Write your five goals and the biblical passages on your piece of posterboard. Then paste your photo somewhere on the poster.

3. Now, go from poster to poster reading everyone's five goals. On each person's poster, write one or two things that you appreciate about him or her. Finally, return to your own poster and embellish it with the creative materials. Take your poster home, tack it on your bedroom wall and read it occasionally as you change and grow through Christ this coming year.

PAPER TOWEL LESSONS

Give youth group members a chance to use their artistic talent while learning about biblical principles.

Give each person a paper towel (the kind that have flower or fruit designs on them) and fine-point colored markers. Ask group members to trace over the designs and add other color and detail to create beautiful art.

After group members complete their artistic paper towels, use the towels as the object for a Bible study on one of these topics:

- Isaiah 40:8—"The grass withers and the flowers fall, but the word of our God stands forever."
- John 15:2—"He cuts off every branch in me that bears no fruit . . ."
- Galatians 5:22-23—the fruit of the Spirit.

God can use fruit, flowers and paper towels to illustrate his love and power.

PEOPLE COLLAGES

This is a good experience to discover how others see us.

Have each group member write his or her name on a slip of paper and place it in a hat. The hat is then passed around and everyone chooses a name other than his or her own.

Then kids each look through old magazines and newspapers and cut out any words or pictures that describe the personality of their chosen person. Have members each create a collage of their person by pasting onto a sheet of construction paper all the pieces they've cut out. Since this is a positive experience, discourage everyone from portraying negative sides of people's personalities.

After everyone is finished, display the posters and see whether the group can guess who is described by each collage. Then have each poster creator explain his or her creation.

PETER AND PEER PRESSURE

Your group will have a great experience with this object lesson.

Begin by studying Peter's response to Jesus walking on the water (Matthew 14:22-33): When Peter knew *who* was calling him, he had the faith to step out of the boat. Com-

pare this to peer pressure—how lots of voices try to influence group members in bad ways, but that they need to wait and listen to God's still, small voice.

Have one kid volunteer to leave the room while the others move around furniture and other objects to set up a maze. Blindfold the volunteer and tell him or her to find his or her way through the maze. Tell the volunteer that your voice will be the "voice of the Lord" and he or she can trust you to tell him or her the right way. When you return to the room, the other group members should shout wrong advice on which way to go. But you should quietly and calmly tell the volunteer how to proceed safely.

Give kids each a turn to find their way through a new maze. Learning to tune out the shouting and listen to the small voice is a great lesson—and fun too.

PRAISING STONES

Here's a vivid illustration of Luke 19:37-40.

Collect tempera paint, brushes, water, bits of felt, scissors, yarn, glue and cotton balls. Give each person a smooth stone (about 1 or 2 inches in diameter).

Have kids sit in a circle; place the craft materials in the center. Instruct group members to paint faces on their stones using the felt and cotton balls for hair. Then read Luke 19:37-40.

Say that no one has actually heard rocks praise God but they're capable of doing it if humans won't. Tell everyone to praise God rather than have the "stones" do it.

For added fun, pass around toothpicks with small squares of paper. Have kids create scripture songs and attach them to their stones with glue or tape. Or vote on the ugliest or prettiest stone. Announce the winner as "The Best Rock of Ages."

PRAYER ADVOCATES

Here's a warm way to share God's love with others in your group.

Form a circle for group prayer. Any person in the group can ask the group for prayers for another person in the group by standing behind that person and placing his or her hands on the shoulders of that person. At that time, anyone in the group may offer a silent or spoken prayer for the designated person. The advocate closes the prayers with an "amen" or a spoken prayer.

PRAYER PARTNERS

Involve adults in the youth ministry and help the teenagers feel really special through a Prayer Partner program.

Recruit adults of all ages who are willing to commit themselves to pray for a teenager for one year. Assign each adult a young person to pray for. Provide basic information about him or her (name, address, age and birthday, hobbies and interests, church involvement). Encourage the adults to send notes, send birthday cards and recognize special achievements.

Keep Prayer Partners secret throughout the year. You will need one person, though, to relay information between the Prayer Partners and the young people. The teenagers may want to correspond with their Prayer Partners about prayer needs or appreciation for cards and notes.

Between Christmas and New Year's Day, hold an evening reception where young people and Prayer Partners meet. It's always a beautiful time when the teenagers learn who their adult "pray-ers" have been.

PRAYER PROBE

For an overnight retreat, use two different prayer exercises to go along with a theme on prayer.

The first one is Cliché Prayers. Break up into small groups and have each group compose a prayer using all of the clichés they have ever heard used in prayers (everything from flowery introductions of God to overworked catch-all

phrases). If your group is small you might want each member to compose a cliché prayer. Then share with the whole group. The results will not only be entertaining, but also effective in pointing out what prayer should not be. You may take it a step further and trade cliché prayers, and then translate them to conversational prayers. Then lead into a discussion on elements of effective prayer.

The second idea is Prayer Bags. Supply each person with magazines and a brown lunch bag. Members then search through the magazines for pictures or words that represent the things they have recently prayed about. They can include things they have been thankful for as well as items they have asked for. Members snip the photos and words and put them in their bags. After everyone has finished have each person share his or her bag with the group, explaining how he or she has used prayer recently.

PSALM 1, ILLUSTRATED

Making a slide presentation from Psalm 1 is an excellent learning project for a youth group.

Begin the project by having a lesson or series of lessons studying the Psalm. Pick out and list all the "picture" words and phrases such as "walk in the counsel of the wicked," "stand in the way of sinners" and "tree planted by streams of water."

Next, go out into the community and/or congregation and take a series of 35mm slides to illustrate the various phrases. For some phrases you might want to take a series of shots.

Then put together a slide presentation. This could take the form of a dramatic reading of the Psalm while the slides are being shown. If some of your members are talented musically, they could put Psalm 1 to music and sing it in coordination with the slides.

Finally, present the slide show to the congregation during a worship service or other church function.

QUESTION OF THE WEEK

To help kids find answers, try Question of the Week.

Have each group member write on a small posterboard a question about problems he or she faces at school, with parents or at church. Then display the posterboard questions and choose one to discuss the next meeting. Have each group member write that question on a 3×5 card.

Tell group members they're each responsible to ask the question of as many people as they can before the next meeting. Youth leaders should do the same. The leaders should also find scripture passages that relate to the question.

During the next meeting, have group members report responses from other people and give their own thoughts and feelings about the question. Next, divide the group into small groups of four to six kids and adult leaders. Read the scripture passages and discuss how the scriptures apply to the question. End the discussion by having the kids give positive responses to the questions.

Have one person in each small group report the small group's responses to everyone.

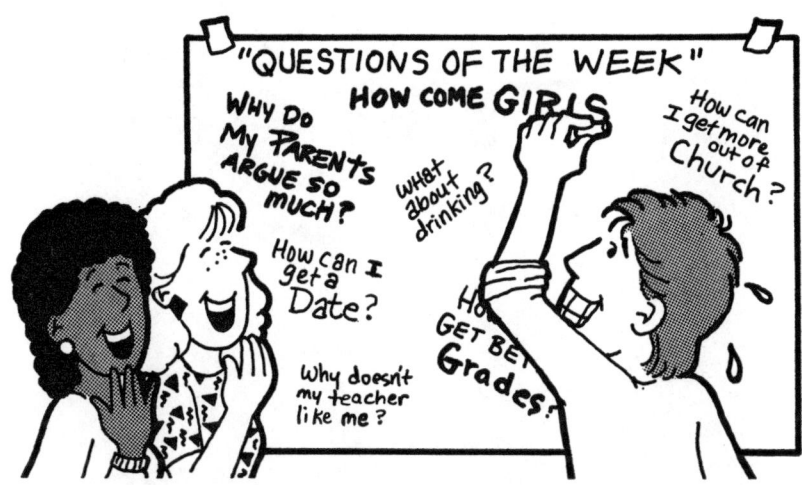

SECRET BIBLE STUDY

After discussing the hardships of Christians in communist nations one Sunday, one group decided to have a Bible study that characterized a meeting behind the Iron Curtain.

No one parked near the home in which the meeting was held. There were no lights on in the house (candles were the only light). The leader arranged to have the meeting interrupted by policemen who pulled up to the house with lights flashing. They pounded on the door and confiscated all the Bibles (this was a surprise to the kids). The kids then went around the room and shared verses of scripture that they had memorized. They finished the meeting by observ-

ing the Lord's Supper.

It made everyone more thankful for their freedom to worship, and more mindful of the persecutions of Christians in other countries.

SELF-IMAGE OBJECTS

This activity helps your group members learn more about each other and themselves as well.

Ask the young people each to bring three objects to the next youth group meeting. One object represents how they think others see them; one shows how they see themselves; and one shows how they would like others to see them.

The objects may be either abstract or concrete. For instance, objects may be poems, pictures, quotations, books or keepsakes.

At the meeting, have each person show his or her objects and explain why he or she chose them.

SENSE SCRIPTURES

Here's an idea to help the Bible touch the senses as well as the intellect. It's a good way to begin Bible study, discussions and informal gatherings.

First, read aloud the selection from the Bible. Then have group members close their eyes. Read the passage aloud again. Ask members to use their imaginations to sense the biblical story by setting themselves in the middle of the story and then telling what they see, hear, smell, taste and feel.

Start with a sense-pounding Bible story such as Jesus calming the sea in Mark 4:35-41. Responses may be the following:

● See—darkness; big, black clouds; lightning; huge waves.

● Hear—thunder; splashing; men screaming; boat creaking.

● Smell—rain; salt; wet people who don't smell good anyway.

● Taste—water; salt; "cottonmouth" caused by fear; lunch coming up.

● Feel—seasick; the boat rocking; humidity; fear; anger

(because Jesus is sleeping); confusion; helplessness.

This process sets the mood for digging into the meaning of the text. The Bible is easier to understand if you can imagine yourself in the middle of it.

SHOPPING MALL ADVENTURES

For a good time and good lessons, take your group to a shopping mall for an afternoon or evening.

Send out group members for the first 45 minutes to shop and enjoy one another's company, but also to observe commercialism as it appears on products and advertisements. Then meet together at a central point to discuss what we're "supposed" to be like according to these ads or products (for example, tall, thin and attractive)—and what God says we should be like (for example, loving, kind and patient).

The next 45 minutes is for studying shoppers—how they act, what their attitudes are, etc. Then meet and compare some generally accepted attitudes toward life (for example, getting) and what Jesus said and how he lived (for example, giving).

Finally, scatter to observe sales clerks. Meet at an ice cream shop this last time and discuss how the clerks seem to see their roles—as servants or bossy-type people? Do they act like they're doing a favor when they offer help or like they really want to help? Together think about servanthood as Christians, and look at examples from Jesus' life.

SOAP CARVING

Soap Carving is easy, simple and a good way to share important symbols in your life.

All you need for each person is a bath-size cake of soap and a paring knife. Have members each carve a cake of soap into a symbol (no matter how simple) of what is important to them right now.

Then, after a set time period, each person explains his or her sculpture and shares why this symbol is important.

Kids may end the experience by giving their symbols to someone else as a tangible way of sharing what they value most.

SPIRIT CARDS

Use Galatians 5:22-23 for a brief study and the focus of a nine-week exercise. For this exercise, give each group member a stack of nine 3×5 cards and a felt-tip marker. Instruct everyone to print a fruit of the Spirit (as found in the passage) on each of the nine cards. Break up and find a place where each person can be alone to pray and ask God to guide his or her judgment.

Then have members spread their cards out in front of them and choose the fruit of the Spirit that they think is developed best in their personalities. Each member takes that card and places it face up in front of himself or herself. Then have members pick the card that stands for what they believe is the second best-developed fruit in their lives. Continue this until the end. You'll have a stack of cards that, from the bottom to the top, contains the fruit of the Spirit from the best to the least developed in members' personal lives. These are their spiritual profiles.

Instruct each member to take his or her cards home and put them in a place where they will be seen several times a day. The cultivation of the fruit written on the top card is the assignment for the week.

Each week as you come together for the youth group meeting, devote a part of your program to a session in which members break up into groups of four or five. Each member of the group identifies his or her top card and rates his or her spiritual progress for the week. Each member offers encouragement to the others. Remove the top card and place it on the bottom of the stack. At this point, each person identifies his or her new top card and that becomes his or her assignment for the next week. Members share how they hope to produce the newly assigned fruit of the Spirit.

Kids get excited about this program. The first question they ask at the meeting is, "What's your top card?" and then, "How are you doing?"

At least two words of caution: First, don't let anyone believe that this exercise will result in spiritual perfection. No one is going to master a fruit of the Spirit in one week. This is only an awakening. Members will be working on the fruit of the Spirit for the rest of their lives. Second, help kids see that they cannot produce these virtues by their own efforts alone. For the fruit of the Spirit are just that—the fruit of God's Spirit dwelling in the Christian's life.

STAND ON NUMBERS

This is a "strength of feeling" exercise.

Pass out paper and pencils. Have each member copy a list of issues such as abortion, politics, school, feminism, censorship, church, police, soap operas, names of singers and TV shows. Each person chooses a number between 1 and 7 that indicates how he or she feels toward each issue. "One" indicates strongly negative feelings and "7" indicates strongly positive feelings.

While kids work on this, place sheets marked 1 through 7 on the floor in a straight line about 2 feet apart.

After members finish ranking each issue, ask them to stand on the number corresponding to the first issue. Have them stand there only a few seconds to look around the room and see where the group stands. Then call the second issue, and continue through the end of the list.

This is a good method to kick off a discussion on any topic.

SYMBOLIC GIFTS

Divide the group into subgroups of about eight people. Then each of the eight should hunt around the church, home or wherever you're meeting for seven items that would make symbolic gifts of love to the other people in the group.

Allow plenty of time for the hunt, perhaps as much as an hour. Give careful thought to the selection of each gift.

For example, cut some paper into little bits, making confetti. This could represent joy for a person in your group who needs some cheering up. Or find a phone book, symbolizing your appreciation to a person in the group who has phoned you when you were lonely.

After everyone has gathered all the gifts he or she intends to give, regroup and sit in a circle. Then, one at a time, each member receives his or her gifts from the seven other members. Have each member explain each gift as he or she gives it to the recipient.

This is a sharing of love. Avoid jokes and gag gifts.

These gifts may be the most beautiful ones you'll receive this Christmas.

TALENT MATCH

Use this game to start off a program on self-esteem. Show your group members that some talents are deeper than visible characteristics.

Send three or more people out of the room. Give everyone else a piece of paper and a marker. Ask the group members to write one thing they do well such as sing, babysit, study or get along with parents. Collect the papers.

One at a time, invite the other group members back into the room and give each 30 seconds (depending on the number of young people) to place the "talent papers" in front of the correct owners. Those correctly matched stand up, and the guesser keeps changing the rest of the papers until the time is up. The person with the greatest number of matches wins.

Talk about the abilities and talents we might overlook but other people notice. Read Matthew 25:14-30 and discuss how we should use all of our talents and abilities.

THINKING OF GOD

Attributing human characteristics to God is called anthropomorphism. God has used this often in the Old Testament when references were made to his hands, voice, feelings, etc. The following are value clarification strategies that can help members understand how they think of God today.

Have each person place an X on the line that represents his or her thinking on the issue.

After everyone has answered all the questions, allow time for discussion and voluntary sharing of answers.

Thinking of God

1. Using human years, how old do you think God would be?
   1 year ———————————————————————— 100 years
2. How do you think God would dress today?
   Modern ———————————————————————— Very formal
3. In your mind, God's mood with you is mostly . . .
   Critical ———————————————————————— Accepting
4. How involved is God in the affairs of people today?
   Passive ———————————————————————— Active
5. If God would speak to you today, what would be the tone of his voice?
   Very soft ———————————————————————— Very forceful
6. God's workload in your mind would be . . .
   Very busy ———————————————————————— Very casual

For the following, circle your answer.

7. If you had something to discuss with God, would you have to make an appointment with him? Yes/No
8. Would you go to God or would he come to you? Go/Come
9. Where would you meet him? His office/Outside in a park
10. How much time would be involved?
    All the time you needed/All the time he had

Permission to photocopy this handout granted for local church use only. Copyright © 1988 by Group Books, Inc., Box 481, Loveland, CO 80539.

THIS IS YOUR LIFE

Plan a fun and memorable night for your youth director or special member by giving him or her a big surprise. This activity works especially well when celebrating a member's or leader's birthday.

This Is Your Life requires careful preparation. First, you must learn about the "celebrity's" past without him or her knowing about your investigation. Find out about important events in his or her life, and gather a few stories that might be a bit embarrassing to the celebrity but funny to the audience.

Arrange for a few old friends, parents and teachers to make surprise appearances in your This Is Your Life meeting.

Then, on the big night, have everyone congregate in your auditorium for a "special meeting." Then your selected master of ceremonies will call your surprise celebrity to the stage. The Emcee then begins telling the story of the celebrity's life. As each highlight is reached, a surprise guest walks on from backstage. If you really want to do a professional job, have each surprise guest say a sentence or two into a microphone before appearing on stage.

You can conclude with a party with cake and ice cream for your celebrity.

This Is Your Life may bring a few humble tears to the eyes of your celebrity, so it's a good idea to have a box of Kleenex handy. This activity is an excellent way for a group to communicate its love for its leader or one of the members.

TOURS FOR TEENAGERS

Career decisions are an important part of a high school student's life. A great way to help older teenagers explore different careers is to tour community businesses. These tours can help young people realize how many different jobs are available and how their special talents and gifts fit into the working world. Call high school counselors or chambers of commerce to find out what tours are available.

At the next youth group meeting, have group members discuss what they learned on the tours. A series of these tours can give young people career information and personal confidence.

TWO GREATEST COMMANDMENTS

Use this service to emphasize the two greatest commandments.

Above the meeting room door, hang a banner that says "Love the Lord Your God With All Your Heart." Above the sanctuary entrance, hang a banner that says "Love Your Neighbor as Yourself." For each group member, fill two communion cups: one with pure water and the other with water and a pinch of salt. Leave these filled cups in the meeting room.

Before the young people enter the meeting room, ask them to wear choir robes and remove their shoes. Say that they are about to enter the Holy of Holies and there is to be no talking or laughing. Inside the room, light a candle

and have each person drink a communion cup filled with water, which represents God's purity. Then have each drink the cup of salt water, which represents our impurity. The message: Even small sins are noticeable to God, yet he commands us to love him with all our heart. He wants our love. Close this portion by saying a liturgical prayer.

Give each young person a lighted candle to carry into the sanctuary. Once inside, sing songs of praise to Jesus for his Resurrection. Discuss how much Jesus loves us and how much we should love others. Ask, "What are some ways we can 'love our neighbor as ourselves'?"

Your youth group will always remember this service *and* the two greatest commandments.

UNEMPLOYMENT LINE

Generate discussion on vocations with this game.

Before your group meets, place a box in the center of the meeting room. On separate pieces of paper write 50 occupations (for example, teacher, lawyer, trash collector, dogcatcher and circus clown). Fold these and put them in the box.

When group members arrive, form four teams and place each in a corner of the room. Explain: "On 'go,' one person from each team runs to the box and picks a piece of paper. He or she runs back to the team and pantomimes the vocation until the team guesses it. The game continues until each person has had a chance to pantomime a job. The first team done wins."

Read Colossians 3:12-17 and discuss the qualities God wants to establish in us—on the job or off.

WHAT'S IMPORTANT?

This exercise helps to decide what's really important in life.

Give everyone five 3×5 cards. Have members each write the five most important things in their life on the cards (one item per card). These can be objects, people, desires, goods, relationships, abilities or whatever. Then ask the following questions:

1. Do any of your cards concern objects such as money, clothes or a car? It has been stolen . . . drop these cards on the floor.

2. Do any of your cards concern relationships with a per-

son of the opposite sex (boyfriend or girlfriend)? That person has just dropped you . . . drop these cards.

3. Do your remaining cards refer to your special talents or abilities such as athletics or music? You've suffered a terrible accident and can no longer use those talents . . . drop these cards.

4. Do your remaining cards have something to do with relatives such as your parents? They've suddenly died . . . drop these cards.

5. Keep any cards you have not dropped. Don't pick up any cards already dropped. Discuss these questions: What cards are in your hand? Could you live with only that? What card was most difficult to drop? How would you feel if you actually lost what you wrote on the cards?

Finally, study Matthew 6:33: "But seek first his kingdom and his righteousness, and all these things will be given to you as well."

YOU WERE THERE

This is a fun Bible study idea.

Choose a topic for Bible study, then pick a place to study.

You Were There Bible studies are easy to imagine. Here are some examples:
- Go to a cemetery and conduct a study on death.
- Lock up the group in a jail to study Paul's imprisonment.
- Go to a hilltop and make an altar for Abraham's near-sacrifice of Isaac.
- Study some of Jesus' healing miracles in a hospital chapel, then split up and visit some of your congregation's ill people.
- Have outdoor surroundings for a study on Psalm 23.
- Study Jesus' birth in a barn or cave.
- Find a desolate area and study Jesus' temptation in the wilderness.
- Take the group to an absolutely dark place for a light/darkness study of 1 John.
- Study the Revelation to John on an island.

Skimming through the Bible reveals all kinds of study ideas. Let curiosity and excitement build for You Were There Bible studies by keeping the topic and place of the study a secret.

"Being there" helps Bible studies come alive. And it's a fun way to learn.

Reaching Out

ACTION ANNOUNCEMENTS

Announcement time is usually when everybody is talking and nobody is listening, right? Well, try something different.

Prior to a youth group meeting, briefly write the pertinent information regarding the announcements on separate pieces of paper and fold them up. Then read through the announcements and decide which method of making the announcements would be most effective, and label it such. On the outside of the folded paper, write the number of participants required to make the announcement.

At the beginning of the meeting, ask for volunteers to help you. (Don't mention what or how they will be helping.) As you glance through the announcements, choose the young people who you feel would do the best job at each of the various methods of announcing. Try to involve six to 10 members in this announcement time. The response is terrific! Have these individuals leave the room for about five minutes of preparation before they present their announcements to the group. Send one or two adult volunteers out of the room with them to help them as they prepare. While these people are out of the room, the rest of the group is singing or doing a crowdbreaker. After about five minutes, call them in one at a time to perform the announcement or demonstrate it to the group.

This announcement time requires audience participation, and people learn and retain longer those things in which they are an active participant.

Some effective methods of demonstrating or performing the announcements are charades, pantomime, news reporting, poetry (making the announcement rhyme) and alternating words (two individuals do the announcement by each reading every other word).

It's exciting and fun! Your group will love it! But don't wear it out—use it maybe once a month or decide what is best for your group.

ANDREW CLUB

To increase youth group enthusiasm and attendance, form an Andrew Club. Andrew was always bringing people to

Jesus—for example, Simon (John 1:40-42), the boy with the loaves and fish (John 6:8-9) and the Greeks (John 12:20-22). A club in his honor would study about Andrew and challenge its members to "bring people to Jesus" too.

Ask interested young people to sign a sheet saying they will try to bring someone new to church (or Bible class or youth group) each month for a year, or a total of 12 times. Host occasional club meetings for members to study together and share successes and failures of being in the Andrew Club.

Every year have a special service or meeting to award official Andrew Club members with Andrew Club T-shirts, jackets, plaques or certificates. This is also an opportunity to read thank-you notes from "visitors" who've become involved with the group because of "Andrew."

Along the same line, you could start a Barnabas Club. "Barnabas" means "one who encourages"; club members would be encouragers by remembering group members' birthdays with cards, cutting out and posting city or school newspaper articles highlighting group members, and regularly writing and sending notes of encouragement.

CARING RAID

It's a raid! Show your love for a needy family, an elderly couple, a lonely widow or even an inactive group member by organizing a Caring Raid.

Arm the members of your raiding party with refreshments, songsheets and a Bible verse or two (1 Corinthians 13 is especially appropriate). Arrive unexpectedly shouting, "We love you—this is a raid!" Spend some time feasting, singing and talking. Be sure not to leave a mess.

Your demonstration of love will be appreciated and remembered for a long time.

CARNIVAL CAN NIGHT

Want a fun activity that will excite your youth group and help a local service organization? Try a Carnival Can Night. This activity features several games: Basketball Shoot, Ring Toss, Balloon Bust and Miniature Golf. Obtain some simple prizes to give away to the winners of the various games. Bubble gum, candy and pens from local businesses make good prizes.

Here is the key to making your Carnival Can Night work. Each game requires a certain number of tickets. Tickets are obtained by trading canned goods. One canned good equals 10 tickets. It's simple! The more canned goods you bring, the more you can play! The more you play, the more prizes you can win!

After your Carnival Can Night is over, donate the canned goods to a local service organization. That organization can provide food for needy families in your community.

CHARITY SCAVENGER HUNT

Brighten the holiday season with a Charity Scavenger Hunt. Collect useful items for a local or denominational shelter for teenagers.

Secure a list of items needed at the home—for example, toothbrushes, toothpaste, combs, soap, shampoo, writing paper, pencils and school supplies.

Advertise the scavenger hunt in the newspaper; hand out fliers to people in the church neighborhood. Let people know which items you're seeking and when kids will collect them for the shelter.

On the day of the hunt, divide the group into teams and assign each team a specific area. Have the teams go door to door in their areas with lists of items they're collecting. In one area, many people purchased items to give scavenger hunters. Some businesses donated items as well.

Award a prize to the team that collects the most items on the list.

Check with the shelter. Perhaps you can take your group to visit and present the gifts in person.

A Charity Scavenger Hunt will teach sharing, give the youth group visibility and bring holiday cheer to less fortunate people.

CHRISTMAS CARD DELIVERY

Since postage is becoming so expensive and people no longer send many Christmas cards, deliver Christmas cards for your congregation free of charge.

Set up boundaries of the delivery area. Make the church the center of your map. In a city, one mile in each direction could be the boundary for your delivery. Stretch the boundary if you live in a rural area.

Give the congregation members two weeks notice as to when the deliveries will be made so they can have their cards in on time. Ask them to put their return address on the envelope in case of a questionable mailing address on the envelope. Make sure the congregation knows the boundaries by giving the people a map that shows the boundaries. Set at least two delivery dates in case you are inundated with mail. Deliver the cards on the two Sunday afternoons before Christmas.

Decorate a big box for people to drop their cards in. Put the box in a convenient location where all can see it.

Divide the cards according to city blocks, districts or whatever is suitable to your surroundings. Cards placed in the box that do not fit into the specified boundaries should be returned to the senders. Divide your group into four smaller groups to cover north, south, east and west districts around the church. Send each district out in the appropriate number of cars. Make one person in each car in charge of seeing that all the mail is delivered. Delivery must take place in a quiet, orderly manner because this is a witness to the neighborhood. Meet back at the church to make sure everyone finishes safely.

Your congregation will greatly appreciate your neighborly and money-saving service.

CHRISTMAS IN JULY

Most nursing homes and rest homes receive group visits at Christmas and Easter, but rarely are they remembered during the rest of the year. With this knowledge, your youth group can set out to surprise the patients of a local nursing home or rest home for the Fourth of July holiday.

Make red, white and blue tray favors: Construct fluted snack cups wrapped in tissue paper and gathered at the top

with a ribbon bow. Insert in each one a religious sticker or symbol and free samples of cologne for the men and perfume for the women.

Your surprise will be like a cool, refreshing breeze during the long, hot summer.

CLIP ART ALBUM

Getting tired of using dogeared clip art every time you publicize a youth group activity? Do you hate the hassle of using envelopes and file folders for clip art? Then why not use a photo album for your clip art collection?

Any photo album that allows for pages to be added to it will work. The clear plastic covering not only keeps your clip art clean and pressed flat, but also helps you find that special piece of artwork faster. Place tabs on the edges to mark special sections such as "seasonal" (spring, summer, winter, fall), "cartoons," "Bible," "quips and quotes" or "camp."

A low-priced photo album makes each piece of artwork last a long time.

COMMERCIAL BREAK

Do you find that newsletter reminders and spoken announcements of upcoming events don't get the attention they deserve? Go video!

Let your group members plan and videotape commercials promoting events for the month ahead. Give everyone a chance to participate as a creative writer, a performer or a member of the production crew.

Limit the video program's length to 10 minutes, and show it during your usual announcement time. Be sure to continue printing reminders of upcoming events in newsletters or church bulletins to keep parents informed of group activities.

COMMERCIALS FOR JESUS

This activity will help your young people consider the importance of sharing their faith.

Create a studio by setting up a VCR, a video camera and a television in one room. In another room, explain to your young people that they're going to make commercials for Jesus. Each person will have 30 seconds to tell what Jesus has done for him or her.

Take group members one at a time into your studio to videotape the commercial. Don't offer ideas. Give the young person a five-second countdown, then start the camera. Signal when 15 seconds have passed, and again when the 30 seconds are up. You should be able to complete about 20 commercials in 30 minutes.

After everyone has been videotaped, show the tape twice. The first showing will give everyone an opportunity to laugh, but the second one will help your group think about what they tell people about Jesus.

CONSTRUCTION SITE ART

Many large construction companies often have to build fences or walls of wood around their sites that are in high traffic areas. Did you know that their public relations offices will often buy paint and brushes if young people will do the designing and painting?

Invite kids from several churches to participate. You'll impress the community, and you might even get radio, TV and newspaper coverage.

Here's how to set it up. After your group decides to look

into the project, contact the construction company public relations department. Persuade the P.R. people to buy the paint and brushes if you'll supply the people. Then members should submit sketches on a given theme such as "Springtime in Atlanta" or "What the World Needs Now Is Love."

When paint day comes, distribute the various colors of paint in paper cups to all your artists. Call the news media. Arrange for the mayor or other official to judge the colorful panels and award prizes.

And you don't need a group full of professional artists. Those members with some artistic talent can be given the job of sketching the large murals—and everyone else simply fills in the blanks with their paints. Beautiful!

DOLLAR BILL GIVEAWAY

You'd think anyone would take a no-strings-attached gift of money, but most people are suspicious or disinterested.

This activity helps your young people understand that sharing their faith can be as difficult as giving money away. This activity can also help prepare your group for a mission trip.

Divide your group into pairs (trios at the most) and take them to a shopping mall. Give each pair one brand-new dollar bill.

The goal is to give the new dollar away. The kids must not offer any explanation or even say they are part of a church group. They must simply give the dollar to a stranger.

Only three places are off-limits: video game rooms, restrooms and Christian bookstores. Set a time limit and designate a meeting place.

Have at least one adult volunteer stay at the meeting place during the exercise to help with any problems. That adult might have a second dollar bill for teams that manage to give their first dollar away.

You might also want to plan an activity for those who finish early. For instance, make arrangements with a Christian bookstore to let the kids listen to Christian music when they finish. Promise the manager careful supervision of the group.

Return to the church for debriefing and worship. Discuss how it feels to be rejected. Help your kids relate this activity to sharing their Christian faith with others and the fear that goes with witnessing. Remind your group that some people readily accept witnessing, some are suspicious, some are angry and some are puzzled.

Close with a time of worship using Christian witness as your theme.

DOUBLE-DUTY GIVING

No doubt you've heard of gift certificates. But did you ever think of sending "Promise for Improved Conduct" certificates as Christmas greetings? Challenge group members to give these!

Have young people fold sheets of construction paper to resemble Christmas cards and paste on Christmas seals or pictures. Have them print "Promise for Improved Conduct" in large letters across the top. Parents will be so shocked when they read those words that they won't be able to wait to look inside.

The message inside might read like this: "Mom, I'm sorry I do so many things that annoy you. This Christmas I want to put the 'peace on Earth' theme to work. I'm going to listen to you more closely, choose my words more carefully and do my part to keep up with the chores. When I fail, I hope you'll pray for me and know that I'm trying my hardest."

Take any other situation that bothers group members and adapt the "Promise for Improved Conduct" to the individual circumstance. If a young person has a problem in school, this is a good way for him or her to show the teacher that he or she wants to change. Young people can also use the certificates for Sunday school teachers and pastors to let them know that they've heard what they are teaching.

By taking such a bold step toward self-improvement, young people can show they mean business.

Encourage group members to follow through with this type of giving; remind them that they'll be in for a surprise. What fun to find a gift that serves double duty. First, kids make someone happy, then they get happy themselves through the joy of giving and the satisfaction of making progress toward a goal.

FEBRUARY LOVE-IN

Here's a way for your young people to show love.

Hold a group meeting at the beginning of February. Have each member choose a scripture passage about love and write it down.

Explain the meeting's purpose: to make a paper chain of love and present it to the congregation.

Have members each write on strips of newsprint their love scripture references. Have kids write Bible references only—not the passages.

Supply Bible concordances so kids can find the exact references if they don't know them by heart. Then let half the kids look up more verses on love and the other half write them on newsprint strips. Play songs about love while kids work. Play games during breaks and serve refreshments.

Tape the strips of newsprint together to form a long chain. Carefully store the chain until the Sunday before Valentine's Day. Then present the chain to your congregation by circling everyone with it; bring together the chain's two ends at the front of the church. As the families leave for home ask them to tear off a scripture verse, look it up and read it with family members.

GARDEN OUTREACH

One youth group tried an idea that turned out great as a ministry and a fun project.

An elderly couple lived near the church. They were having problems with weeds taking over their back yard. In the past they'd kept a large vegetable garden, but were no longer able to maintain it because of health problems. So the youth group asked for permission to clean up the yard and plant a new vegetable garden. The kids told the old folks they could keep any of the produce they wanted, and members would give the rest to the shut-ins of their church.

The couple liked their idea. So group members began planting and caring for the garden. They eventually harvested squash, cucumbers, carrots, eggplant, pumpkins and string beans.

Every Wednesday they piled themselves and a load of vegetables into their church van and visited shut-ins. These sweet people really appreciated the fresh produce. But, even more than the food, they enjoyed the brief visits with the youth group.

Whenever kids had an oversupply of vegetables, they'd take them to the City Rescue Mission.

This project was successful not only to the shut-ins and the City Rescue Mission, but also to the elderly owners of the garden site. The project gave them the joy of watching their garden being used and kept up, gave them something to look forward to, and filled their back yard with jovial young people with whom to talk and laugh. And the positive influence on the kids was greatly enriching too.

A GIFT OF LOVE

A Christmas Gift of Love need not be limited to the yuletide calendar. The spirit of Christmas goes beyond its particular religious significance—it means giving, sharing and getting in return. It means giving of yourself and experiencing the love of friends.

Give group members each a piece of paper and have them divide it into four columns. In the first column, have them list their five closest friends and three to five close family members.

In the second column, have kids list the gifts they gave these people last Christmas. These should be material gifts.

In the third column, have kids list a gift of the Spirit that they would like to give each of these people. It should be a special, intangible quality such as love, kindness or patience.

In the fourth column, ask members to list a gift that each of these people might give them based on their close knowledge of the kids. Members should ask themselves, "What quality would each of these people like to see in me?" The answers to this question could tell the kids something useful about themselves, their friends and family and their relationships with them.

Say: "You can help other people achieve their goals by giving them what you think they want. But most importantly, you can help them achieve their goals by giving them the year-round gift of love: friendship."

GROUP GREETING CARDS

This simple idea promotes group spirit and a sense of caring among members. You'll need 11 large sheets of paper or posterboard, and bright-colored markers.

Print one letter of the phrase "Get Well Soon" on each sheet. Have group members huddle together holding the letters and photograph the group. Have many prints made.

When a group member or friend is ill, have everyone sign

a get-well card and send it along with the group photo.

Also use this idea to send other messages: "Happy Birthday," "Have a Fun Trip" or "We Miss You" to a member who hasn't attended group meetings for a while. The possibilities are endless.

HALLOWEEN TREAT NIGHT

On Halloween night, give out treats and friendship to the older and shut-in people of your community.

Ask people in the congregation to bring candy and baked goods to the church the Sunday before Halloween. Compile a list of people in your church and community who might

benefit from a friendly visit on Halloween night. Then, on Halloween, canvass the area—visit people, sing to them and leave goodies. A party back at church finishes off a fun Halloween.

An interesting variation for Halloween Treat Night might be to distribute food and clothes to needy families.

HIGH-TECH SLIDES

Here's a quick and easy way to use personal computers to make announcement slides with excellent graphics. You'll need a personal computer with word-processing software and a 35mm single-lens reflex camera.

Simply type into the computer the words you want so

that on the screen they look exactly like you want the slide to look. Take a picture of the screen: Use a tripod to steady the camera, and artificial light (for example, a strobe). Set the shutter speed to 1/60 second, and use standard 64- or 100-ASA slide film.

With a little imagination, you'll be making creative, high-tech slides in no time.

HUNGER GAME

The complexities of world hunger can be explored in this fun game.

Divide into teams of six to eight people. Have each member choose a prepared name tag: "farmer," "grain dealer," "government official," "Russian merchant," "starving Ethiopian," "consumer and taxpayer" and "church leader." Drop the Russian merchant for teams of six; add another farmer for eight.

Each member will need an equal amount of play money, except for the Ethiopian and farmer who will receive no money.

Give the farmer a small bag of popcorn, each kernel representing 100,000 bushels of grain.

Members may wheel and deal with each other in their teams however they wish. And the government official may levy taxes at any time (the Russian and church leader are tax-exempt).

Everyone should know that the score will be taken at the end of 20 minutes. At that time, have each member rate his or her satisfaction with the proceedings on a scale of 1 to 10 (with 10 being ecstasy). Ask members each to write their rating on their name tag. Post the tags by teams and total. The highest score "wins."

Discuss the experience.

HUNGER SERVICE

Host a youth-led worship service based on hunger in the world.

Divide the pews in the church into geographical areas of

the world—South America, North America, Asia, Africa and Europe. Reserve three rows for Europe, five for North America, 18 for Asia, and so on. Then seat the congregation according to each area's population. Put 15 people in each European row, five in each North American row, and so on. The congregation members can feel how crowded or spacious their world area is.

During the service, a young person represents each world area, talking back and forth with the other world representatives. "Why don't the people over in Asia get themselves a job?" one representative might ask. "Well, why don't you people in North America share more of your resources?" You'll have some touching speeches.

Sing songs related to hunger. Show films too.

For communion, give each world area bread and grape juice (or wine) in the ratios of how much food (per person) their area really has today. Give Asia a half-loaf of bread to share among everyone. Give North America four loaves. It is interesting to watch the sharing start to happen.

JAIL HOUSE BLUES

Jail House Blues is a great activity to attract new members and excite the regulars.

Everyone arrives dressed in "rough criminal" costumes. As each arrives, take instant-print "mug shots" with criminal numbers. Also take group shots in front of a height-marked police line-up background.

After photos, take thumb prints. Occasionally say: "This one looks like the type who would cut off her thumbs! We better print all her fingers (or toes)." Interrogate everyone under a hot light, writing name, address, phone, school, hobbies and other information.

After booking the "crooks," hold a Kangaroo Court in which each member receives sentencing for some "dastardly" crime. Then send the criminals to jail for "bread and water" (refreshments).

This is a great time to pass out calendars of youth activities for the coming year or quarter. You may also want to come together for a devotion on Paul's imprisonment. Check your local public library for a short Keystone Kops flick.

Use Jail House Blues as a kickoff program for your fall meetings. Retreats would also be a good setting for the activity. However used, Jail House Blues builds relationships and provides a photo and lots of information on each group member and visitor.

LOVE SONGS

Want to get inactive members back in the youth group? Try adding this ingredient to your next youth visitation adventure to homes of your inactives. This is especially fun around Christmas.

Have the whole group go "caroling" together. Use tunes of favorite Christmas carols and add new lyrics. A carol might go something like this:

We missed you on Sunday morning,
We missed you on Sunday morning,
We missed you on Sunday morning and Sunday night too.
Good tidings we bring of our next youth fling,
Good tidings from Christians who really do care!
(Sung to the tune of "We Wish You a Merry Christmas.")

Why not raid the refrigerator while you talk to the inactive member about upcoming youth events?

MAP FOR LOST MEMBERS

Try this one on any of your members who have dropped out of activities.

Send the inactive member a personalized map, showing how to get to the church from his or her house. Add all

sorts of funny or interesting details on the route. Include a note explaining that you assumed the missing member had forgotten how to get to the church.

Also add a sincere note that you really do miss this person and you'd like to see him or her active again.

MIRROR MESSAGES

How can you get publicity mailings to reflect that an event will be fun?

Draw a funny-looking face on a piece of paper and cut eye holes. On the other side, write your greeting and introductory message, instructing the readers to look through the eye holes at a mirror to get the rest of the message.

On the funny-face side, carefully write your important event news *backward*.

Your group members are sure to get a laugh—and to read the event publicity information.

NEWSLETTER PIZZA CONTEST

Do you ever wonder whether your teenagers read the youth group newsletter?

If so, then have a contest to challenge them to read it for typing errors. The first 10 who find a typo in the monthly newsletter win a free pizza meal with their youth minister.

Use an answering machine to get an accurate "first 10" count.

This works for many reasons:
- The kids will read the newsletter.
- Going out for pizza with the kids helps you get to know them better.
- Going out for pizza also helps 10 diverse kids get to know each other better.
- It keeps you humble; the kids find more errors than you plan.

NURSING HOME PET SHOW

Here's a different twist to nursing home ministry. Why not put on a pet show?

Many nursing home residents adopt a small pet—a rabbit, dog or cat. Sometimes the Humane Society visits nursing homes and brings animals for the residents to enjoy.

Your youth group can do this too. Call a local nursing home to set up a time and date for your pet show. Have kids bring their family pets. Those who don't have a pet to bring can borrow one from a friend. Prepare the pets for display (bathe, groom and dress them). Make sure dogs and cats have leashes, turtles have boxes and rabbits have cages.

At the nursing home, have each young person tell his or her name and the pet's name. Have each share a brief pet biography: how it got its name; how long the young person has had the pet; what it likes to eat; the personality of the pet; and the funniest thing it's done. After each young person has shared, let an elderly resident see the pet up close—to touch, hold, look at and talk to. If the pet show is a success, arrange to have one on a regular basis: monthly, quarterly or semiannually.

The event creates a unique bond between the elderly and the young. In fact, some of the kids may go back on their own to visit the home.

OUTDOOR EASTER DECORATIONS

It's not uncommon to decorate outdoors during the Christmas season—so why not do the same for Easter?

Have youth group members decide how to decorate. Will you use balloons, banners, posters, streamers, ribbon, kites, giant butterflies, windsocks or giant kiosks? Collect, construct or buy the decorations. Some stores, businesses and individuals may be happy to donate or loan certain items. Ask your church boards to donate some money to help with costs. It's okay to make an investment because you can use the decorations from year to year.

Recruit a few early birds to put up all the decorations on Easter morning before the first church service. That usually means *before* sunrise. Attach your decorations to tree limbs, light poles, church steps, railings or the church itself. Create a celebration of color, movement and new life!

And here's a way to involve the entire congregation in the act. Make and distribute Easter "kits." Fill lunch sacks with decoration "ingredients"—balloons, assorted crepe paper streamers, string and a butterfly pattern. Include suggestions and instructions such as a banner idea, new-life Bible verses or an explanation of different Easter symbols. Suggest that planning and decorating be a family project. Ask all church families to display their decorations outside their homes on Easter morning.

This artistic activity can be a powerful witness to the entire community. It says that the church and the Resurrection victory are not just on the corner of Sixth and Vine—but everywhere God's people live!

PALM SUNDAY FAIR

While searching for a new way to learn about Lent and the events of Holy Week, one group hit upon the idea of a Lent event that they called a Palm Sunday Fair.

They spent the Sunday class periods from Ash Wednesday to Palm Sunday preparing for the event. They prepared collages depicting the words "Crucifixion" and "Resurrection" and displayed the collages along with cinquain poetry about Lent written by group members—to publicize the coming event to the congregation.

Then they prepared games that would teach others about Lent and Holy Week.

Grades three through eight were invited to join the group on Palm Sunday during their regular church school hour to participate in the fair. Adults and younger children of the congregation joined the group during the fellowship hour after the class.

Teaching games included a Bingo-type game highlighting scripture passages associated with the events of Lent and Holy Week; a board game that lighted up when the correct answer was given to questions about the symbols for Holy Week; and a picture game in which the pictures had to be put in chronological order to show the order of events during Holy Week. The picture game utilized the line drawings from *Good News for Modern Man*. The drawings were projected onto a wall with an opaque projector and redrawn by group members. (Be sure to get permission from the publisher before doing this.)

Posterboards were hung from the ceiling. Each posterboard represented an important day during Lent from Ash Wednesday to Easter Sunday. Details about a particular day were spelled out on the posterboards so that the younger children who had not participated in the study could get answers to their questions.

Films on Lent from the American Bible Society were shown.

A food booth served foods of the Holy Land that the youth group had researched.

Group members served as facilitators during the fair by helping the younger children play the games, running projectors, serving food and keeping things running smoothly.

The Palm Sunday Fair was a success from every point of view. Group members learned a great deal while preparing for the fair, and the children and adults learned by coming to the fair.

PANTRY RAID

Here's a fun way to gather food for distribution to the needy. Organize a Pantry Raid.

Three weeks prior to the raid, begin announcements in Sunday morning church and in the church newsletter. Inform the congregation that your youth group will be coming around to "raid" everyone's pantries.

When raid night comes, pairs of members scatter to the homes of church members. At each house the members ask the resident to rummage through the pantry to find some canned or boxed food to donate to the needy. One partner hands out pamphlets explaining the purpose, while the other partner carries a box for collecting the food.

PHONE DEVOTIONS

Do your young people have trouble with their daily devotions? Do they spend too much time on the phone? Consider this.

Set up a daily devotional phone line. A young person can call and listen to an upbeat, 2½-minute devotion. Record a new message every day on the church's answering machine(s). In addition, give a phone number where you can be reached for those who want to talk with someone.

Promote this by blitzing your local schools and concerts with sharp-looking business-size cards that display the phone number and theme, "A dynamite call for a lift." Many "outside" kids who won't come to a church will call for the message. A particular series on suicide, for example, may result in many kids calling for help and finding it.

You'll see an additional impact on your youth group members too. On weekends they could take turns telling about their faith life or giving a brief devotion on the tape. They could tell their friends to call, and thus become more bold in their Christian witness.

At the end of the message briefly give the details of your upcoming events.

It takes some work to pull this off well, but it will be worth the effort!

PHOTO REVUE

Here's a great way to build group spirit and have a few laughs. Assign someone in your group to be the group photographer. Have this person take pictures (slides) of all your group activities over a three-month period.

Then, every three months have a big slide show. Keep the show moving at a good pace, and be sure to include plenty of funny shots.

This activity promotes your program by showing different activities. And it gives a responsible job to your youth photographer. Plus, it's a fun time that your members will really look forward to.

PHOTO TEAMS

Ask several kids to bring instant-print cameras. Form teams; once each team has a camera, the only limitation is its ability to be imaginative and creative.

Here are some ideas to get you started into the world of youth group photography:
- Illustrate a passage of scripture using photos.
- Create a cartoon-strip story where photos replace the cartoons. Write captions to tell the story.
- Develop a storybook for young children by using photos instead of artwork. Print the story in large letters.
- Illustrate a specific theme you'll be studying.
- Photograph everyone's eyes, noses, ears, knees or feet

and make a creative poster to publicize your group at church.
- Using a balcony as a platform, photograph a message that's written below. People spell out the words by using their bodies to form letters.
- Have people in the team photograph things that tell others about themselves (hobbies, interests, likes, dislikes).
- Have a photo scavenger hunt. Each team tries to photograph all items on a list.

PIZZA PIG-OUT

This activity is a fun way to build attendance in your group.

Plan to have a Pizza Pig-Out during a regular youth group meeting. Tell kids to expect free pizza and to invite their friends.

Buy a roll of tickets and give group members each five— one for themselves and for four extra guests. Everyone who attends the pig-out must have a ticket.

Make sure group members tell guests the date, time and place of the pig-out. Because of a larger group, a larger meeting place may be needed.

Order pizzas from one of the kids' favorite places. Figure three slices per person. Have plenty of paper napkins and plastic forks on hand. Supply drinks.

When kids and their guests arrive at the pig-out, ask them to each write their name, address and phone number on the back of their ticket. Collect tickets. Use the information to follow up on visitors; have door prizes and draw tickets to choose winners.

Use a fund raiser to cover the cost of the pig-out. The free pizza will draw lots of new kids to your group.

POSTER DAY

Get your group into a big picture: a poster. Call all members, inactives, boyfriends and girlfriends. Put an ad in the church newsletter. Search the highways, byways and arcades. Shout it from the mountaintops, treetops and table tops that Poster Day is coming.

Ask a member in your church to take several snapshots of your "mob." Send one of the photos to a company that enlarges photographs into full-size posters. (Ads for these companies can be found in several magazines such as Seventeen.)

Hang the posters in the meeting room, give them as gifts and even sell a few. Poster Day goes over so well that you may plan to make it an annual event.

A variation of this activity is to use a 35mm camera and black-and-white film. Gather the kids for a group photo. The developed prints are the size of a post card. Add a greeting to the bottom of the photo with press-on letters from a local art store. Mail the post cards to your kids for any reason: birthday wishes, get-well wishes, wish-you-were-here messages.

PROGRESSIVE PUBLICITY

How do you publicize an event or activity so that everyone becomes interested?

Let's say you need to publicize a study of the Old and New Testament titled "Something Old, Something New."

One month in advance, place the letters "SOSN" on small

pieces of paper around the church. The next week add the date of the Bible study. Then the next week insert the time and place, until eventually all the information is added.

Everyone has fun figuring out what the letters "SOSN" stand for and trying to guess the upcoming activity.

As a result of this publicity, group members will have more interest and more people will attend the Bible study.

PUBLICITY POSTERS

Here's a simple but effective way to publicize an upcoming group event.

Arouse curiosity by posting several large posters where they'll be well-seen. Each poster should carry one of the following words (in big letters): "What?" "Where?" "Who?" "How?" "When?" "Why?" and "Why Not?"

Leave these posters up for a week or so, then write in the details on each.

This method really draws attention and feeds upon people's natural curiosity.

PUMPKIN SYMBOLS

What activity could be more "cut out" for Halloween than pumpkin carving?

Add a creative idea to a youth group pumpkin-carving party: Slice Christian words or symbols instead of faces in the pumpkins.

You'll need sharp knives, old newspapers, candles, plenty of pumpkins and lots of enthusiastic carvers.

Ask each person to carve a Christian word or symbol that's especially meaningful to him or her.

End the evening with a candlelight worship service in the church. Place candles inside the pumpkins and arrange your carved works of art throughout the sanctuary. Display pumpkins on the pulpit, altar, floor—wherever. The soft, orange glow shining through the words creates a special worshipful atmosphere.

Speak of God's Spirit shining through each person (see Galatians 5:22-23). For a reminder that each person is the light of the world, refer to Matthew 5:14-16. Or if you want to emphasize Jesus as the light, read John 1:1-14.

For a seedy snack—wash, salt and roast the pumpkin seeds in a low-temperature oven. Serve them for an after-carving snack!

Encourage young people to take their masterpieces home. Suggest displaying them in their windows as a shining Christian witness!

REASONS OR EXCUSES?

Try this to ignite a discussion on church attendance. Ask each group member to write five good reasons for attending church. Have members compare, discuss and then rank the reasons from "best" to "worst."

Next ask each group member to write five good reasons for *not* attending church. Encourage them to list ones they've used, they hope to use, they know friends use, and others they think are worth mentioning. Again compare, discuss and rank the reasons.

When members discuss the reasons in light of Hebrews 10:25, they discover that some of the reasons gradually become excuses.

What a discussion!

ROSTER

One of the most effective tools in a youth group is also one of the simplest—a Roster.

Obtain each member's name, address and phone number, and photocopy the list. The size of your group makes no difference. Both leaders and members will use this Roster often. Make sure everyone has a copy.

When you need to notify everybody for a special meeting or activity, use the Roster as a "pass it on" phone list. The leader calls the first kid on the list with the message. That kid calls the next person and so on. If the kid below your name is not home, you should call the following name—then, at a later time, call the name below yours again. In this way, your group message won't get hung up somewhere. You may want to print the "pass it on" instructions at the top of the Roster.

Also, the Roster works well for chain-letter communication. For a special group event, the first kid on the list sends a personal letter to the next person—with instructions that the letter must be sent to the next person or the chain will be broken. Each person adds a personal note to the letter and sends it on to the next group member. You should include a Roster in the envelope in case one of your members has lost his or her copy. The chain letter should be started well in advance of the event you're promoting.

Everybody likes mail and phone calls from friends, so these two ideas are sure winners.

The Roster also tends to re-excite kids who may have drifted away from the group. They're kept posted of your activities, and there's a good chance they'll return.

Update your Roster often by adding the names of new members and making address corrections. Make sure everyone gets a new copy.

ROVING PHOTO SCREENS

A pleasing effect for your next worship service or multimedia program is quite easy to perform.

Construct one or more screens-on-a-stick. A large piece of white cardboard tacked to a long stick will do.

Now project your slides or movies onto the screens held by the group members. The screens can be moved about to create interesting effects.

The projector can be left stationary while the screen moves left, right, up and down—catching the projected image as it passes. The screen can also be moved closer to the projector—"zooming in" on one portion of the image. Or the projectionist can follow the screen as it moves.

Members can achieve a dazzling effect by using several

projectors and several screens, all roving about the room catching images everywhere.

SANTA'S SECRET SERVICE

Not the night before Christmas, but 10 nights before, begin this activity.

Have group members pretend they belong to Santa's Secret Service and choose one or more special families to surprise. The special family might be well-liked, motherless or fatherless, new to the neighborhood or have a handicapped member.

Each of the 10 nights before Christmas, Santa's Secret Service leaves a small wrapped gift at the special family's

front door. (Gifts can include cookies, jam, holly, a huge homemade Christmas card, a gift certificate, Christmas napkins, a red candle.)

Leave the gifts at different times each evening, ring the doorbell and run!

The special family will ask everyone, "Who's leaving these gifts at our door?" But Santa's Secret Service members keep their secret and gleefully plan their next surprise!

SIGNED, ANONYMOUS

The U.S. Postal Service can be your ally in creating interest in activities at your church. Approximately five weeks before a special youth group event, send cards to teenagers who are associated with your church but don't normally attend youth functions. Let's say the event is the showing of a film titled *The Question* on May 15 at the church. The cards will simply say "May 15" and not be signed.

The next three weeks, do the same; send unsigned cards with the date. Use a different type of card for each mailing. Change-of-address post cards from the post office or cards from local motels will do fine.

The week before the event, use official church letterhead or post cards to send a signed message that reads something like this:

May 15: Sound familiar?

May 15: Film, *The Question*

May 15: The Fireside Room at (church's name and address)

May 15: Be there

This approach adds to the church's postage expense, but also adds interest among kids. And that's worth the investment.

SNAPSHOT BROWSER

Keep a youth group photo album in which snapshots of members' participation in various activities form a pictorial history of your group.

When someone is interested in joining your group, a look through your album is an ideal way to show what you're all about.

SOFA STUFF

This idea encourages better youth attendance for mid-

week evening meetings.

During a meeting, have all of your young people pile on the sofa. Take a photo of the group, preferably with an instant-print camera. Hang the photo over the sofa and include the date and total number of kids who were present.

Your group members will soon be talking about breaking the Sofa Stuff record.

Within weeks of the start of Sofa Stuff photos, your average attendance is likely to increase.

SPONSOR A CHILD

Send a disadvantaged child to school, feed a hungry child or provide medical care to a needy child.

All you need to do is have your group members commit themselves to bringing a set amount of money to each meeting. If you have 20 members and each brings just 25 cents per week, in a month you'll have $20. That amount can go toward providing the necessary services for a needy child overseas.

Ask a group member to collect the money each week and

send it off at the end of the month.

Some of the organizations that can set you up in sponsoring a child are the following:
- Christian Children's Fund, Inc., Box 26511, Richmond, VA 23261.
- Compassion International, Box 7000, Colorado Springs, CO 80933.
- Food for the Hungry, Inc., Box E, Scottsdale, AZ 85252.
- World Vision, 919 W. Huntington Dr., Monrovia, CA 91016.

With a bit of commitment and prayer your group can make a significant impact in our troubled world.

SUPERMINUTE

Your group can design one of the most powerful and touching minutes of your church's Easter service. Have interested group members interview on cassette tape people in the church and community answering the questions "What does Easter mean to you?" and "Describe an Easter that you remember as being really meaningful or happy to you." Be sure to interview small children as well as adults.

Play the tapes back to the group and choose the best remarks. Be sure to keep track of which comments are on what tapes. Use recorders with counters if you have them. Next, arrange the comments in a logical or interesting sequence.

Then use another cassette player and blank tape to record

the various comments in the order you want them.

On Easter, play the tape for the rest of the church using the church's sound system.

Use the Superminute concept for other occasions or celebrations. (For instance, on Mother's Day record little kids describing their mommies.)

TREE SANTAS

You can bring a lot of joy to disadvantaged families in your area this Christmas with little expense.

Visit the Christmas tree lots in your area and see if the owners will agree to let your group have all their leftover trees on Christmas Eve or before.

Obtain from a local social service office, or perhaps your church, a list of all those families in your area that cannot afford a Christmas tree.

Then, when you get your truckload of trees, get together and deliver a Christmas tree to each of the needy families. They'll be surprised—and grateful.

TRICK-OR-TREAT REVERSED

The kids in your group probably have gained a good deal from the people in your congregation and neighborhood. Most likely they have carted away a couple of truckloads of trick-or-treat candy.

Here's an idea your group can use to return some of that goodness back to your neighborhood. When you go Christmas caroling, take along sacks of Christmas candies and cookies. After you've sung your song on the doorstep, give the people inside a sack of goodies. This is a fine act of love and Christmas giving.

You can have a lot of fun getting together before your caroling party, too, by baking and decorating cookies and candies.

TUTOR SERVICE

Homework? Everyone needs help with that!

Meet on a Saturday to plan the project. Have all members choose a subject they like. Plan to work with elementary school students because the homework is easier to decipher. Ask a local high school counselor to talk to the youth group about tutoring methods. After a general discussion, ask the counselor to talk about the special problems of tutoring each school subject that members have chosen.

Hold the tutoring session from 3 to 5 p.m. one day a week at the church. Ask members to donate one day (at least) each month. Make sure you have enough members to represent each of the main subjects each week.

Announce the project in the church bulletin. Parents sign up after the Sunday service at a special booth and agree to donate money for each session to help fund future youth group projects. Parents also agree to drop off their children at the church for their tutoring sessions and pick them up at 5 p.m.

This project benefits the members of the church. Children's grades improve. Even tutors' schoolwork improves, since each lesson is a basic review of their earlier education. Both parents and school officials appreciate the project. Tutor Service also serves to unify the church and its members as they work together to help the youngest members.

"WHO'S HIS" NEWS

Boost youth group morale, get more visibility and help church members get better acquainted with group members—run a regular "Who's His" section in the church newsletter or bulletin.

Send parents "student profile" sheets that ask for basic information about their young people: grade, school, activities, interests, honors and awards. Ask for confidential information about how the parents view their young people's spiritual lives.

Prepare a "Who's His" logo to help recognize this new, regular section.

Feature one or two group members per newsletter or

bulletin. Let the "who" be a surprise.

Your group members will love this! They get to know each other better, and the ones in the limelight really get a lift (and wonder where you got all that information).

YOUTH BREAKFAST WEEK

Hold a Youth Breakfast Week this spring. Invite all the junior and senior highers from your county, town or school district to meet weekdays before school from 6:30 to 8 for breakfast. Invite an inspirational Christian speaker or musician. The event brings churches of all backgrounds to work together and communicate their care for young people.

Here's how to do it. Hold the program at your church. You and/or the associate pastor of your church begin booking speakers and musicians in September and wrap up the plans before Christmas. After the new year, develop a theme and inform the speakers and musicians.

Have your youth group do the publicity.

Ask an adult volunteer to recruit other churches to assist in planning breakfast menus and food orders. Have volunteers from a different church prepare breakfast each morning during the breakfast week.

Churches involved in this event raise money to cover the expenses for the food, speakers and musicians. Encourage churches to donate buses to transport kids to their schools following the event each morning.

This program will go over so well with the kids and the community that everyone will want to have an annual Youth Breakfast Week.

YOUR IDEAS WANTED

Have you participated in a fun, original youth group activity? GROUP Magazine is on the lookout for creative, unique youth group games, parties, retreats, discussions, special events, worship ideas and fund raisers.

If your group has an idea, submit it to the following address:

**"Try This One"
GROUP Magazine
Box 481
Loveland, CO 80539**

You will receive a check for every idea we publish.

Contributors to *Group Growers*

Jon Adams
Mary Albert
Rick Allen
Ron Almberg
Annette Andrews
David A. Ashworth
Susan Atkinson
Esther M. Bailey
Gwyn Baker
Tommy Baker
Garry Baldwin
Janet Balmforth
Barry Barrios
Robert L. Beasley
Bob Bensonhaver
Mark C. Bigley
Bryan Blomker
Bill Blue
Ron Bodager
John H. Boller
Paul Borthwick
Beth Boyd
Jeff Boyd
Will Boyd
Lee Bracey
Burt Brock
Monica A. Brown
Robert Brown
Terry Caouette
Bryan Carter
Rick Chromey
Renee Coffee
John Collins
Ray Cooper
Richard Cooper
Sam Crabtree
Bob Cross
Karen Darling
Bill Davis
Glenn Davis
Richard Davis

Susan Echaore-Yoon
Jim Emerson
Jane Erickson
Daniel G. Felts
John Filler
Mary Kay Fitzpatrick
Dorothy Forman
Paul Freeman
Steven French
Gil Garcia
Frankie Garrick
Norma Gibbs
Jeff Graham
GROUP Staff
Jim Gullett
Kim Hall
Jeff Hanna
Terry Harp
Karen Hartman
David Hatfield
Carl Heine
David R. Helms
John W. Herron
Michael Hofferber
Tim Holland
Tim Hollard
Will Horton
Lee Hovel
Bill Hubbard
David B. Ingram
C. Daniel Jessee
Darrel M. Johnsen
Jim Lemons
William H. Levering
Philip Lewis
Judy Lindhag
Mark Lundborg
Diane Luton
Leo Lytle
Dave Mahoney
S.J. Marinella

Sherry Mast
Ben Mathes
Gary N. McCluskey
Dan McGill
Glenn Megill
Gloria Menke
Sam Miller
Sue Moore
Gary Moran
Timothy Morrison
Paul Mullen
Karen Musitano
Virginia Myers
Doug Newhouse
Steve Newton
Alton R. Noblett
Linda K. Oliver
Mitchell Olson
Linda Owens
Wayne Pauluk
Cindy Peterson
Lois Peterson
Eric Preibisius
Phil Print
Jim Pritchett
Charlotte Randall
Rob Raynor
Shirley-Raye Redmond
Colleen Reece
Durand Robinson
Laura Rushton
Sharon Saine
John Schluep
Hope Scurry

Mark Seanor
David Shaheen
Ben Sharpton
Margaret Shauers
Barb Silcox
Dave Silvey
Sam Simpson
Sheri Simpson
Cathy Skogen
Mike Slater
Morris Slingluff
Katherine Smithberger
John Stumbo
Douglas L. Suggs
Jeff Swedenburg
David Taylor
Paul Taylor
Gail Thomas
Jean Marie Tognotti
Mike Townsend
Trinity Lutheran Church,
Hudson, Wisconsin
Waneen Tulloch
Wanda Vassallo
Vickie Waddell
John Ward
Paul Warder
Ernestine Weaver
Douglas Weddle
Paul E. Wedlock
Scott Welch
D. Ray Wiggins
Carlos Wilton
Michael Yengo

More ministry-building resources from

Quick Crowdbreakers and Games for Youth Groups

from the editors of Group Publishing

Get over 200 sure-fire meeting openers for your group. Here's a collection of powerful icebreakers guaranteed to get meetings, retreats and lock-ins off to a lively start.

These dandy crowdbreakers get all your kids involved fast. And they're ready in an instant. Simply pick a mixer and start playing.

Kids will get involved fast with—
    Knee Sit   Towel Soccer
    Back Art   Cinderella Shoe Match
    Bumper Bods   Chuckle Chain

Plus scores of other action-packed ideas. Add spice to any youth gathering, large or small, with fun activities from **Quick Crowdbreakers and Games for Youth Groups.**

ISBN 0931-529-46-8, $8.95

Fund Raisers That Work

from the editors of Group Publishing

Meet your group's fund-raising goals with this profitable new resource. You'll get scores of fun money-making ideas that really pay off.

Discover tips for successful fund raising—and turn your ideas into cash. Teach kids how to provide services and products people want and need. You'll get loads of secrets for successful fund raising, including . . .

- ▶ The dos and don'ts of fund raising
- ▶ Fast fund raisers—ideal for busy leaders and kids
- ▶ Proven publicity ideas
- ▶ Handy planning tips, and more!

All 83 fund-raising ideas have been successfully tested by youth groups across the nation. **Fund Raisers That Work** is a collection of the best ideas from GROUP Magazine's popular "Try This One" section.

ISBN 0931-529-33-6, $7.95

Building Community in Youth Groups
by Denny Rydberg

Get practical ideas to help you transform your collection of young people into a close-knit, caring group. **Building Community in Youth Groups** shows you how to:

- Establish trust within your youth group
- Help kids listen to each other
- Change "me" attitudes to "we" attitudes
- Challenge young people to grow spiritually
- Create opportunities for members to care for each other

Discover more than 100 creative activities and discussion ideas to help you replace barriers between young people with Christlike caring.

ISBN 0931-529-06-9, $11.95

Instant Programs for Youth Groups 1, 2, 3
from the editors of Group Publishing

Get loads of quick-and-easy program ideas you can prepare in a flash.

Each meeting gives you everything you need for a dynamic program. Step-by-step instructions. Material lists of easy-to-find items. Dynamic discussion starters. And ready-to-copy handouts.

Each book gives you 17 (or more) meeting ideas in topics that matter to teenagers . . .

    1—Self-Image, Pressures, Living as a Christian
    2—Me and God, Responsibility, Emotions
    3—Friends, Parents, Dating and Sex

With all three books, you can keep a year's worth of program ideas at your fingertips.

Instant Programs for Youth Groups 1, ISBN 0931-529-32-8, $7.95
Instant Programs for Youth Groups 2, ISBN 0931-529-42-5, $7.95
Instant Programs for Youth Groups 3, ISBN 0931-529-43-3, $7.95

Youth Ministry Care Cards

Here's a fast, inexpensive way to keep in touch with your kids. **Youth Ministry Care Cards** are crazy, colorful post cards with special messages to lift the spirits of any teenager. Each 30-card pack contains six wild, original designs. Send your kids . . .

- Affirmations—upbeat, positive messages of encouragement
- Attendance Builders—attract more kids to your youth ministry events

There's room to jot a short, personal note. Plus, Bible verses on each card to strengthen your message. You'll turn any day into a special day with **Youth Ministry Care Cards**.

Affirmations—ISBN 0931-529-28-X
Attendance Builders—ISBN 0931-529-36-0

These and other Group books are available at your local Christian bookstore. Or order direct from the publisher. Write Group Books, Box 481, Loveland, CO 80539. Please add $2.50 for postage and handling. Colorado residents add 3% sales tax.

More ministry-building resources from

Quick Crowdbreakers and Games for Youth Groups

from the editors of Group Publishing

Get over 200 sure-fire meeting openers for your group. Here's a collection of powerful icebreakers guaranteed to get meetings, retreats and lock-ins off to a lively start.

These dandy crowdbreakers get all your kids involved fast. And they're ready in an instant. Simply pick a mixer and start playing.

Kids will get involved fast with—
- Knee Sit
- Back Art
- Bumper Bods
- Towel Soccer
- Cinderella Shoe Match
- Chuckle Chain

Plus scores of other action-packed ideas. Add spice to any youth gathering, large or small, with fun activities from **Quick Crowdbreakers and Games for Youth Groups**.

ISBN 0931-529-46-8, $8.95

Fund Raisers That Work

from the editors of Group Publishing

Meet your group's fund-raising goals with this profitable new resource. You'll get scores of fun money-making ideas that really pay off.

Discover tips for successful fund raising—and turn your ideas into cash. Teach kids how to provide services and products people want and need. You'll get loads of secrets for successful fund raising, including . . .
- ▶ The dos and don'ts of fund raising
- ▶ Fast fund raisers—ideal for busy leaders and kids
- ▶ Proven publicity ideas
- ▶ Handy planning tips, and more!

All 83 fund-raising ideas have been successfully tested by youth groups across the nation. **Fund Raisers That Work** is a collection of the best ideas from GROUP Magazine's popular "Try This One" section.

ISBN 0931-529-33-6, $7.95

Building Community in Youth Groups

by Denny Rydberg

Get practical ideas to help you transform your collection of young people into a close-knit, caring group. **Building Community in Youth Groups** shows you how to:

- Establish trust within your youth group
- Help kids listen to each other
- Change "me" attitudes to "we" attitudes
- Challenge young people to grow spiritually
- Create opportunities for members to care for each other

Discover more than 100 creative activities and discussion ideas to help you replace barriers between young people with Christlike caring.

ISBN 0931-529-06-9, $11.95

Instant Programs for Youth Groups 1, 2, 3

from the editors of Group Publishing

Get loads of quick-and-easy program ideas you can prepare in a flash.

Each meeting gives you everything you need for a dynamic program. Step-by-step instructions. Material lists of easy-to-find items. Dynamic discussion starters. And ready-to-copy handouts.

Each book gives you 17 (or more) meeting ideas in topics that matter to teenagers . . .

    1—Self-Image, Pressures, Living as a Christian
    2—Me and God, Responsibility, Emotions
    3—Friends, Parents, Dating and Sex

With all three books, you can keep a year's worth of program ideas at your fingertips.

Instant Programs for Youth Groups 1, ISBN 0931-529-32-8, $7.95
Instant Programs for Youth Groups 2, ISBN 0931-529-42-5, $7.95
Instant Programs for Youth Groups 3, ISBN 0931-529-43-3, $7.95

Youth Ministry Care Cards

Here's a fast, inexpensive way to keep in touch with your kids. **Youth Ministry Care Cards** are crazy, colorful post cards with special messages to lift the spirits of any teenager. Each 30-card pack contains six wild, original designs. Send your kids . . .

- Affirmations—upbeat, positive messages of encouragement
- Attendance Builders—attract more kids to your youth ministry events

There's room to jot a short, personal note. Plus, Bible verses on each card to strengthen your message. You'll turn any day into a special day with **Youth Ministry Care Cards.**

Affirmations—ISBN 0931-529-28-X
Attendance Builders—ISBN 0931-529-36-0

These and other Group books are available at your local Christian bookstore. Or order direct from the publisher. Write Group Books, Box 481, Loveland, CO 80539. Please add $2.50 for postage and handling. Colorado residents add 3% sales tax.